The Knowledge

Management and Leadership from A to Z

Incorporating "Zen and the Art of Cathedral Building"

The Knowledge

Management and Leadership from A to Z

Incorporating "Zen and the Art of Cathedral Building"

Carl Taylor

- • 26 topics relevant to all managers and leaders
- • 26 exercises to benefit all teams
- • 26 perspectives to assist all organizations

Published by The Knowledge Biz

website: www.theknowledge.biz

ISBN 978-0-9565510-0-9

SAN 0162671

EAN/GLN 5030670162673

A catalogue record for this book is available from the British Library

Prepared and printed by:

York Publishing Services Ltd
64 Hallfield Road
Layerthorpe
York YO31 7ZQ
Tel: +44 (0)1904 431213

Website: www.yps-publishing.co.uk

To Alison, Yazmin and Scarlett

Contents

List of figures

Acknowledgements

The story of the Sagrada Familia building project has evolved from 15 years of experience in developing managers and leaders from a wide range of European organizations. As a consequence, I wish to acknowledge the inspiring contributions of many colleagues whose questions helped me refine the story.

The writings of Suzanne Turner (2002) and Steven ten Have et al. (2003) were a source of further inspiration. Their efficient presentation of a wide range of management models gave me the vision for the A to Z sections. By reviewing the first draft of this work, Cliff Kimber provided valuable feedback that helped me see the forest for the trees. And my family's enthusiasm for this project was invaluable.

Finally, thanks are offered posthumously to Antoni Gaudi i Cornet, for reasons that will become obvious.

About the author

Born in London, Carl's early career spanned research in marine science, corporate strategic planning, internal consultancy and new ventures development – all within the Shell International Group of Companies. Following his assignment in new ventures, Carl took an 18-month sabbatical and ran a business development agency in Kent. This opened his eyes to the realities of leading and managing a non-corporate small enterprise. On returning to the corporate fold, Carl formed part of a team leading the development of a Shell/Philips joint venture. In 1990 he made the decision to move into independent working and has provided consultancy, executive coaching and leadership programmes to an extensive client list. Other activities include lecturing in systemic leadership and organization development with a leading UK Business School, and two non-executive directorships – one with an international manufacturing firm and the other with a national Housing Association. Carl lives in Kent with his wife and two children.

Introduction

This practical handbook for personal, professional and organizational development begins with a story. Why? Because stories offer us a means to see and understand our individual worlds in new and enlightened ways. If you doubt this, reflect for a few moments on some of the stories from your childhood that affected you. The sources of these may have been books, films, plays or the spoken words of significant people in your life. I have no doubt that you'll be able to identify at least one story that has been significant to your development.

'Zen and the Art of Cathedral Building' is the story of the building of the Sagrada Familia, or Gaudi Cathedral, in Barcelona. This story, which is part truth, part fiction, offers you a chance to think about management and leadership from a range of different perspectives. You can zoom in on the operational details or take the long view of the strategic content depending on your interests or current needs. You can then explore your own management and leadership challenges through the A to Z sections of the book, which link explicitly with the opening story. The A to Z sections contain a range of models which I have selected for their value in meeting the challenges of modern management and leadership. These models are:

- Described in brief to promote uncluttered learning

- Related to the opening story to promote deeper understanding

- The foundation for 26 exercises to promote individual, team and organization development.

I could have chosen a different mix of models and concepts for this section. Indeed, I spent a long weekend with a large sheet of paper exploring different options. In the end, I made this particular choice on the basis of what I judge to be of greatest relevance to 21st-century organizations as I have experienced them. In these sections you will find an eclectic mix of the old and the new. This eclecticism is further reflected in the bibliography.

The Knowledge website (www.theknowledge.biz) provides an opportunity for you to further explore the material contained in this resource and points the way to additional learning and supporting material. There is also a readers' forum which provides an opportunity to engage with others as you make progress on our journey.

In summary, The Knowledge resources will:

- Make a range of management, leadership and organization development models accessible and memorable to a large population of managers and leaders

- Help readers explore their attitudes and behaviours at work from a range of different perspectives

- Illustrate that many of the problems within our organizational lives are neither new nor unique

- Enhance the creativity we are all able to apply to our management and leadership roles.

Developing yourself as an effective learner

A great deal of research has been carried out over the past thirty years into the way that people learn. One of the key theories to emerge is that of David Kolb (1984), which focuses on the idea of learning by doing. This is highly relevant to managers and leaders working in organizations as by far our most significant learning and development opportunities come from the experiences we have on a day-to-day basis.

Kolb's learning cycle (see Figure 1) is based on the idea that we are formed and modified through experience. The cycle requires four stages to take place for learning to be fully effective:

- Concrete experience – we need to be involved in new experiences

- Reflective observation – we must take time to reflect on our experiences from different perspectives

- Abstract conceptualization – we must be able to form and process ideas and integrate them into logical theories

- Active experimentation – we need to use theories to solve problems, make decisions and test theories, thus extending our concrete experience.

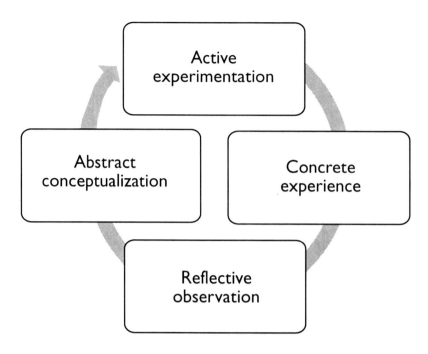

Figure 1: Kolb's learning cycle

By adopting a structured approach to our learning and development we can make the most of our experiences. This is an idea that has had currency for many centuries in the practices of the professional guilds where the process of learning is represented by the apprentice–journeyman–master practitioner tradition. But experiential learning will only be effective if:

- We are open to the learning opportunities

- We are able to make sense of our experiences

- We are able to assimilate our learning into new practices and behaviours.

In planning The Knowledge I had these principles firmly in mind. My aim was to provide a range of mechanisms that would engage users in the learning cycle to the fullest extent. The product is a resource that begins with an apocryphal tale and is then organized around an A to Z of management and leadership, each part of which contains the following components:

Insight

The opening to each A to Z section lifts a sentence or phrase from the main text of that section. This is intended to capture a single insight or point for your own reflective consideration and thereby serve as a primer for what is to follow. Sometimes these insights are no more than simple statements of common sense. However, I find that common sense is not always that common!

Personal reflection

This component offers some of my personal experiences around each concept. In essence, they are my reflections on my journey and in part explain the choice of concepts I've included. In addition I hope they provide an encouragement for you to engage in your own personal reflections.

Model or concept

Here the key theme for the section is outlined by drawing on material from the published literature on management, leadership and organization development. This is the theoretical content that underpins our journey through the resources.

In-depth exploration of the opening story

In this section the model or concept is related back to the opening story of the Sagrada Familia building project, i.e. there are 26 perspectives on this particular case study. Within each perspective many more interpretations are possible.

Team exercise

Herein lies the practical component of The Knowledge, i.e. 26 exercises to benefit all individuals and teams. The exercises are described in step-by-step terms and require little by way of materials or additional resources.

Linking the pieces

Although each section stands alone and is of value in its own right, each model or key concept links to many others. Indeed, if I had made all the links I could imagine, I would simply have linked everything with everything else – thus extinguishing light from the exercise. So, I've restricted myself to just a few suggestions which build seamlessly on the concept in hand.

By organizing The Knowledge in this way, I have produced a multifaceted resource that will supplement your journey to becoming a master practitioner of management and leadership.

Notes on the practical exercises

The individual and team exercises described in the A to Z sections provide the opportunity for you and your team to apply all of the available 26 concepts and models. For simplicity, they have been designed to require no more than the following:

- An A1 flipchart pad

- A supply of flipchart pens in various colours

- Masking tape or something similar to attach flipchart pages to walls

- Adhesive notes

- The collective motivation to succeed.

If possible, all activities should take place off-site in a light and spacious room set up in cabaret style. This will facilitate uninterrupted and productive group learning. But if all you have is some time tagged on to a team meeting in the office, that's better than nothing!

With all team exercises you should feel confident that your team has appropriate levels of trust, honesty and respect as a foundation for its explorations. If in doubt, first carry out the exercises on your own to identify potential areas of sensitivity. Beyond this cautionary point, I wish you fun, inspiration and a wave of creativity.

The characters in the opening story

You will encounter five main characters in 'Zen and the Art of Cathedral Building'. The manager is nameless – because she could be you! Wayne is waning; Payne is a pain; Sayne appears to be the embodiment of sanity; and Jayne is ... well, I'll let you draw your own conclusions. Each character is intended to be an archetype of people we have all encountered in the workplace.

Zen and the Art of Cathedral Building –
An apocryphal tale

Our exploration of management and leadership begins at the site of one of the longest-running building projects of the past two centuries, that of the Sagrada Familia, or Gaudi Cathedral. Antoni Gaudi was one of the most important architects of the Art Nouveau period and his work in and around the city of Barcelona took the Art Nouveau style further than that of any of his contemporaries. The Sagrada Familia is by far the greatest and best known of Gaudi's buildings. Gaudi first presented his design for the cathedral in November 1883 and the building work began under his direction in 1884.

As the project progressed, Gaudi became so committed to this grand design that he spent his final years living exclusively in the workshops surrounding the building site, taking on the appearance of a vagrant. On 7th June 1926, aged 74, he was hit by a number 30 tram on Gran Via de les Corts Catalanes. He died three days later in a pauper's hospital, having not been recognized at the site of the accident.

Gaudi envisaged that the Sagrada Familia would be the finest structure in the Christian world and more than eighty years after his death the project attracts more than two million paying visitors each year. Many of those visiting return over and over again to observe progress on this remarkable icon of the Art Nouveau movement. In 1999 the Vatican agreed in record-breaking time to begin the process of establishing Antoni Gaudi as a saint, an issue surrounded by much controversy and still unresolved.

And now to the present …

Our story begins on a 21st-century spring day in Barcelona. La Rambla was just coming to life and a new construction manager was starting her first day on the Sagrada Familia building project. As she made her way along Carrer de Mallorca, first the cranes and then the ornamental spires of the cathedral came into view. As she approached the entrance to the cathedral, she decided to stop for a coffee at the Pastisseria Bomboniera and reflect on how she should approach her first day in the new job. Having reflected, she decided that it was important to get to know her new team members as soon as possible. She finished her coffee and made her way past the blue tapes at the entrance of the cathedral and on through the great iron gates that separated construction workers from tourists.

On entering the site, she passed pleasantries with some of her new construction management colleagues and then set about getting to know her new team. First, she introduced herself to Wayne and asked him to give her an overview of his job. Wayne mumbled his reply, 'What do I do? That's simple enough. I use a chisel and mallet to turn roughly quarried rocks into rectangular building blocks.' 'Mmm, right,' said the manager, feeling that this wasn't going quite the way she'd expected. Wayne continued, 'And when this lump of rock has the right shape and dimensions I stack it with the others, get another piece of rock and start the whole process again. And I do that all day.' 'Okay,' said the manager, wishing she hadn't started this conversation. 'Oh, there's more,' insisted Wayne. 'When that pile of rocks over there is just about used up, a truck comes round the corner and dumps a whole load more.' The manager politely excused herself and moved on to introduce herself to Payne.

'Good morning, Payne. I'm the new construction manager. I'm introducing myself to the team and finding out what you all do.' 'Ah, I'm a master stonemason,' said Payne with obvious pride. 'You see that template block over there, the one everyone else is copying at the moment? Well, I made that – to within 2mm tolerances of the architect's plan and with perfect 90 degree angles.' 'Impressive job, Payne,' the manager replied. 'Oh, thanks, but that's not all. When I'm not making templates from the architect's plans, I reproduce the current block as part of the manufacturing effort – to within 5mm tolerances and maintaining perfect 90 degree angles.' 'Sounds like you're doing a fantastic job, Payne,' replied the manager. 'It's going to be a pleasure working with you.'

Next came Sayne. His response to the manager's introduction was to say, simply, 'I'm a member of the stonemasonry team.' The manager replied with a simple 'Thanks Sayne, it's a pleasure meeting you.'

Finally the manager reached Jayne, who saw her coming. 'Good morning! You must be the new construction manager,' Jayne began. 'That's right! I'm introducing myself to the team and making a first pass at understanding what you all do.' 'Excellent! Well, I'm building a cathedral, and what's more it's going to be the most fantastic cathedral in the world – just as Gaudi intended.' Pleased at hearing Jayne's obvious enthusiasm, the manager responded by saying she was looking forward to working with her and she then set off to find her new office and continue her first day's work.

Over the next few weeks the manager looked through staff records and monitored the output and quality of her team's work. It didn't take long for a clear pattern of performance to emerge, so she compiled the information into a table to aid her analysis and began to reflect on what to do about the results.

Required performance		Actual Performance			
		Wayne	Payne	Sayne	Jayne
Accuracy for production of blocks	Size to be + or – 10mm when compared to the current template being copied	+ or – 10mm	+ or – 5mm	+ or – 8mm	+ or – 15mm
Rate for production of blocks	10 blocks to be produced per person per day	10 blocks per day	8 blocks per day	11 blocks per day	15 blocks per day
Sickness absence	More than 8 days a year is seen to constitute an issue	24 days	5 days	3 days	0 days

Figure 2: Stonemasons' performance data

A month or so passed and one Saturday morning, while driving through the suburbs of Barcelona, the manager came across a newly opened DIY superstore. Walking around the store, she was attracted to a bright orange sign saying 'Carbon neutral mallets – half the price and twice the durability of traditional wooden mallets'. On looking closer the manager discovered that the mallets were made from recycled plastic bottles discarded by some of the four million tourists that visit Barcelona every year. She couldn't resist. First, there was the appeal of recycled materials. She was currently working on a research project for her MBA entitled *Sustainable Construction Methods in the 21st Century*. Second, she had been tasked by the cathedral's Board of Trustees to cut construction costs. With no hesitation, she bought four mallets.

On her return to work the following Monday, she first approached Wayne and enthusiastically described her new find. But Wayne's reaction was far from enthusiastic. 'Have you seen the size of the latest delivery of rocks? And now you want me to use a new mallet as well. That's it, I'm off.' And off Wayne went on two weeks' sickness absence, supposedly with a repetitive strain injury to his wrist.

Cautiously, the manager approached Payne and said she had some new mallets she'd like the stonemasonry team to try out. 'Why's that, then?' Payne asked. The manager explained that these new mallets were half the price of traditional mallets and twice as durable. Payne inspected the mallet that was handed to him. 'These look like they're made of plastic.' 'Well, they are. They're made from recycled plastic bottles that tourists drop. These will help us reduce our carbon footprint and cut our costs.' 'Oh, I get it,' said Payne. 'Cost cutting. People have been saying you've been brought in to cut costs. So we're now expected to start using inferior tools.' 'Not inferior tools,' replied the manager. 'Ecologically and economically sound tools. These are the future.' Picking up his mallet, Payne said, 'I represent the fourth generation of master stonemasons in my family and all of us have used the traditional tools of the trade. I inherited this mallet from my father and he inherited it from his father. This mallet is a craftsman's mallet. I've had it for over thirty years.' 'Thirty years!' said the manager. 'How can that be? We get through dozens of mallets every year.' 'Well,' responded Payne. 'When I say the same mallet, it's had quite a few new heads and a few new handles – but it's a professional mallet all the same.' With a sigh, the manager suggested that Payne work with the new mallet and she'd see how he was getting on in a week or so. Payne clearly disapproved but didn't respond further.

Sayne showed an instant interest in the new mallets, observing that they certainly looked good but that the balance wasn't quite the same as the ones he was used to. He then went on to say he'd be glad to give the new mallets a go and see how they worked out in practice. Relieved to hear the first positive response from a member of her team, the manager thanked Sayne.

There was no need for caution when approaching Jayne. 'Aren't those the mallets on sale in the new DIY superstore?' Jayne asked. 'Half the price and twice the durability?' 'That's right,' said the manager. 'Using these will make a big impact on our tools budget over the next couple of years.' 'So there'll be more money to be used on employing extra stonemasons,' Jayne continued enthusiastically. 'Something like that,' said the manager – again relieved to hear a positive response from one of her team. Jayne had no problems adjusting to the new mallets.

A couple of months passed and it was time for the manager to go on her annual summer holiday. On the advice of a friend, she booked herself a week in Royal Tunbridge Wells. She wasn't disappointed. The Pantiles' restaurants served a good breakfast and there were plenty of opportunities for her to indulge her interest in looking around old churches. But she was disappointed to see the poor condition of most of the churches she visited. The one outstanding exception was the church opposite the Town Hall. The stonework was immaculate, the stained glass windows sparkled and the surrounding gardens were beautifully cultivated. And on stepping inside she was in for a further surprise. Instead of the usual open architecture, the interior of the church was separated into discrete areas. Close to the entrance there was a coffee bar, galleries along each side of the building displayed the work of local artists, and within an impressive central area a group of actors were rehearsing for that evening's performance of Romeo and Juliet. Confused by all of this, the manager asked to speak to whoever was in charge. The events co-ordinator joined her and, following introductions, the manager heard the story of the Church of the Holy Trinity.

'Many of the churches in and around Tunbridge Wells were built in the mid-1800s, thanks to local philanthropists. This was the first one, designed by Decimus Burton. Most of the parish churches have fallen into disrepair now, though, because of falling attendances.' 'But what prompted such a fine church to be used as it is now?' asked the manager. The events co-ordinator continued. 'In the mid-1970s Holy Trinity was threatened with demolition, so a large number of residents raised a petition to save the church. There were some heated public meetings, but then in 1976 the Church Commissioners approved the Civic Society's proposal to restore the building and convert it to an arts and performance centre, and the rest, as they say, is history. So we now have the Trinity Arts Centre.' 'That's really interesting,' said the manager. 'But what makes it so successful? Are the people of Tunbridge Wells really that keen on the arts?' 'That's a different story,' continued the events co-ordinator. 'In Georgian times, Tunbridge Wells was the place to be seen in. People could mix with royalty and the aristocracy who came for the Chalybeate Spring waters down in the Pantiles and it's still a popular place for tourists to visit, especially as it's so close to London. So the Arts Centre benefits from this.'

Captivated by the creativity and entrepreneurial sense that was embodied within the Trinity Arts Centre concept, the manager continued her holiday by visiting London, with a particular focus on some of the well-known sites designed by Decimus Burton.

When the manager's week-long vacation came to an end she began the journey home. During the flight, she reflected on the Trinity Arts Centre with a feeling of unease. It took a while for her to pinpoint the reason for this, but as the plane circled over Barcelona prior to landing she looked down on the city and the cause slowly surfaced. Work on the Sagrada Familia had begun over 125 years ago and Catalonian society had moved on a long way since then. Barcelona has many parish churches, a significant proportion of which have fallen into disrepair because of falling congregations and a corresponding lack of funds. Given all of this, was she managing a redundant project? She decided to carry out some research when she arrived home.

Over the two months that followed, the manager spent much of her leisure time visiting parish churches across the city. She saw first hand the sparseness of many congregations and questioned people about their views regarding the Sagrada Familia. Would they and their families attend the new cathedral? The typical response was 'No way!' Those questioned went on to explain that their families had been attending these particular churches for generations and they were aware of the threats they faced from falling church attendance. They would continue to attend the parish churches and, moreover, promote further attendance at these churches whenever and wherever they could. It did indeed seem that the Sagrada Familia was in danger of becoming a white elephant!

Reflecting on this further, the manager prepared a presentation for the cathedral's Board of Trustees and called an Exceptional General Meeting. With all members present, the manager began her PowerPoint presentation by detailing the evolution of demographics in Barcelona over the past hundred years. She then presented a tabulated summary of findings from the research she had carried out over the previous two months and projected the potential future income of the Sagrada Familia based on this data. She finished with some thought-provoking questions regarding the potential viability of a cathedral-building project that was due for completion in 2025.

The members of the Board of Trustees were shocked and reactions were varied.

'Why hasn't anyone thought of this before?'

'I've always said we should stop the building work. We should leave it as it is – as a tribute.'

'We're tasked with getting the cathedral completed, not with getting involved in this sort of thing.'

'I think things have already gone pear-shaped. Look at the new façade!'

'Gaudi's intentions were clear and that makes our job clear.'

'Don't worry. This is still going to be a fantastic building – everything will be fine.'

'Are you sure you've got your facts straight?'

Once these outbursts had died down, the manager continued with the second part of her presentation. This detailed how many tourists visited Barcelona, the annual peaks and troughs, the facilities available and, most critically, the potential benefits of having a world-class venue for the visual and performing arts. The trustees listened on. 'Given the size and designed acoustic qualities of our planned cathedral, it would take just a modest change in direction to build the greatest theatre and arts centre in Europe.' With this, the trustees suffered their second shock of the evening. One trustee said passionately, 'It may be a modest change in direction from a builder's perspective, but it's an enormous change in perspective from Gaudi's vision of the finest structure in the Christian world.' But the manager had done her homework.

'Well, is it such a great leap? If we get back to the basics of Gaudi's intention, it was to provide the people of Barcelona with the means to celebrate their faith. The Sagrada Familia was to be a thriving community – a community that would fill the cathedral with its presence. But, over a hundred and twenty years later, many of Barcelona's parish churches are falling into disrepair, largely as a result of falling attendances.' Nobody disputed her words so she continued. 'Gaudi would not have wanted his great cathedral to fall victim to social change. An empty cathedral would serve no purpose. What's more, he was a man of his times, an innovator and active participant in the modernist movement, which was all about accepting and working with change.'

The manager was on a roll now. 'Organic structure and functionalism were the foundations of the Art Nouveau philosophy and there will be little function in a cathedral that doesn't have enough people to provide a sustainable congregation or a sustainable source of income.' The audience was primed for her finale. 'What Gaudi wanted at its most basic level, his core vision if you like, was to provide the means for people to celebrate their Christian faith in Barcelona. What we're seeing in this great city of ours is an erosion of facilities for people to celebrate their faith. If we create the Antoni Gaudi i Cornet Arts and Performance Centre of Barcelona, this world-class project will without doubt become the most successful arts venue in Europe, if not the world.' The trustees were captivated. 'And we can have the best of all worlds here,' the manager continued. 'In honour of Gaudi's vision, 25 per cent of the profits generated by this grand design can be allocated to a new Gaudi Arts and Performance Centre Trust to be used for the maintenance and improvement of Barcelona's numerous parish churches. In this way, a way that is sensitive to the vast changes we have seen in faith and society since Gaudi's tragic death, we will be able to further his vision and place our city at the centre of the world's cultural stage.' She added detailed financial projections based on the new concept showing clearly the income that could be allocated to the maintenance of Barcelona's parish churches. The trustees were so inspired by the manager's presentation that they voted unanimously to make the arts and performance centre a reality.

The manager went into work the following day in high spirits to tell her team. First, she approached Wayne. 'Hello, Wayne, good news. We're no longer building a cathedral, we're building an arts and performance centre. And it's going to be the greatest of its kind in Europe – if not the world.' 'What!' responded Wayne. 'Have you seen the latest delivery of rocks? You want me to cope with that lot *and* build an arts centre?' 'Arts and performance centre,' corrected the manager. This was a step too far for Wayne. 'That's it, I'm off.' And with that, he was off for two weeks, supposedly with back strain.

The manager approached Payne. 'Good morning, Payne. We're changing our plans and building an arts and performance centre instead of a cathedral.' 'And what effect is that going to have on us?' asked Payne. The manager responded by saying that the project architect was drawing up some modifications to the internal structure and there was likely to be an additional entrance area, galleries down the sides and a stage constructed at the centre of the building. Payne started to engage with the manager enthusiastically. 'Sounds as though quite a lot of new building blocks are going to be needed. When the revised plans are finished let me see them and I'll start getting my head around the production of the templates. I expect you'll be wanting the usual 2mm tolerances on those.' 'Absolutely,' responded the manager.

She then approached Sayne and told him of the change of plan. Sayne challenged the manager by saying, 'So, arts and performance centres are the new cathedrals!' Defensively, the manager said that her research had led to that conclusion. Sayne went on to express an interest in seeing the research. The manager agreed to show him the results and moved on to approach Jayne.

'How did the meeting go with the trustees last night?' Jayne asked. 'Really well. They've agreed plans to create *the Antoni Gaudi i Cornet Arts and Performance Centre*,' responded the manager. Jayne gave a very cool reception to this news, but the manager was not overly concerned. After all, Jayne was consistently her most enthusiastic stonemason.

It came as a great surprise when, two weeks later, Jayne gave in her notice.

'But why?' the manager asked. 'You're our most committed and enthusiastic stonemason.' 'I was *committed* and *enthusiastic* about building the Sagrada Familia, not some arts and performance centre that simply bears Gaudi's name. For the past ten years I've been bringing my children here, showing them how we've been getting on. We were going to adopt the Sagrada Familia as *our family* church. And for the next hundred generations, our family members were going to be christened, married and buried in this cathedral. And now you tell me it's going to be some theatre attraction, a money spinner for the city. Sorry, I'm not interested. I'm going to spend the rest of my professional life working on my local parish church, leaving it in a better condition than I find it.' And with that, Jayne left.

A hour later, Payne too gave in his notice. 'And you can keep your plastic mallets!' was his final comment.

On her way home that evening the manager started to reflect on the growing list of issues that now needed her urgent attention. First was that of recruiting some new stonemasons, and traditional stonemasons were in short supply. Second was that of Wayne's sickness absence which had taken a significant turn for the worse of late. Third was finding the time to get back to Sayne on his question regarding her research – and she was starting to feel uneasy about that. Fourth was an issue of planning permission. According to a report in the newspaper El Pais, it was surfacing that Barcelona's planning officials had never responded to two requests to change the plans for the cathedral, one in 1916 and the other in 1990. It seemed someone was beginning to stir up some trouble. Finally, there was breaking news that the construction of a high-speed train tunnel could threaten the foundations of the Sagrada Familia. Giant tunnelling machines were due to bore a 40ft-wide tunnel through the sandy, waterlogged earth passing within yards of the cathedral's foundations. A group of surveyors and geologists were concerned that this may cause subsidence or flooding. The manager's honeymoon period was clearly over.

Postscript

Before engaging with the A to Z sections that follow, you might reflect on a few general points from our story.

- Where do you think the manager showed good judgement?

- Where was her judgement poor?

- Specifically, what would you have done differently?

Putting in the time to noting your responses to these questions at this time is not necessary, but it may enhance your experience of the sections that follow.

A

 An organization's most important asset is its **aspiration**.

Aspiration

Aspiration *n*. A strong desire to achieve something.

 At the age of ten I had a strong desire to be a zoologist, inspired by Gerald Durrell's book A Zoo in my Luggage. At the age of twelve I wanted to become a surgeon, having stumbled across a well-illustrated biology book. Next, I wanted to become a psychologist, having been influenced by a 'significant other' in my late teens. As it happened, I studied biochemistry – the logical choice given my A level results! Now I see a similar journey being undertaken by my children: a dancer last year, a teacher this year and, I suspect, a park ranger next year. These aspirations act as a powerful driver to behaviour – for as long as they endure. My aspirations didn't stabilize until I was in my late twenties when, having worked as an environmental scientist in Shell Research I took a secondment into Shell International's strategic planning team. I became inspired to build my own consultancy business. The business followed six years later. The important lesson I learned from my journey was that aspirations must be well-formulated and enduring if they are to be a long-term asset.

With the UK government's drive during the mid-1990s for organizations to gain the 'Investor in People' award, the buzz phrase 'An organization's most important asset is its people' emerged. I worked extensively with organizations to achieve and re-achieve this award and that experience convinced me of an alternative view. An organization's most important asset is its aspiration – assuming the aspiration is clearly stated and enduring. Thereafter, it is the degree to which an organization's people share these aspirations at a personal level that determines how much of an asset they are. If employees don't have shared aspirations they may become the organization's greatest liability!

The aspiration of an organization is typically stated as a vision or mission statement (we'll explore the differences between these later). Examples are:

- To provide affordable high quality homes

- To give everyone access to the internet

- To deliver services that improve our clients' capabilities to succeed.

The strength of an individual's desire to achieve comes from three elements: how clear they are about what they want to achieve, how realistic it is for them to achieve it, and how much they value achieving it. These elements combined determine a person's level of drive, or motivation. This can be summed up as:

$$\text{Motivation} = \text{Clarity} + \text{Reality} + \text{Value}$$

This summary equation will now form the basis for our exploration of aspiration, first within the context of 'Zen and the Art of Cathedral Building' and then with an exercise for you to facilitate with your team.

Referring to our opening story, we begin our exploration of aspiration with the most tricky case: Wayne. His aspirations are entirely unclear from the information we have about him. His behaviour would suggest he aspires to little more than doing the minimum required to keep his job. As we explore the opening story further, a rich source of ideas will emerge as to what might be going on for Wayne. But for the present we'll accept that he has withdrawn significantly from his job and there is little indication of what drives or motivates him. As such, it is debatable how much of an asset he is to the organization.

Payne's aspirations, on the other hand, are clearly indicated by the data the manager collected. His drive is exclusively towards creating near-perfect building blocks while failing to meet his quantity target, an issue the manager fails to address. Indeed, Payne is so engaged with his trade that I could imagine he has a pile of back copies of *The Master Stonemason's Times* in his bathroom! He probably meets once a month with his master stonemason friends to talk about the depressing loss of quality the industry is suffering and how traditional values are being replaced by modern requirements for efficiency and economy. Payne has not engaged with the required balance between accuracy and productivity. We might feel confident that Payne has the necessary skills to meet the quantitative target for his work, i.e. ten blocks per day at +/− 10mm tolerances, but he chooses to achieve eight blocks a day at +/− 5mm tolerances. And when Payne's professional identity is threatened by the introduction of plastic mallets, the insult to his values becomes too much for him and he resigns. Payne is clearly not an enduring asset to his organization!

We have some clues regarding Sayne's aspirations. He's a member of the stonemasonry team who maintains a healthy interest in new initiatives. As such, he appears to be well aligned with the requirements of being a 21st-century stonemason.

Jayne reveals her aspiration very clearly from the start, i.e. to get the cathedral built as soon as possible. This is reflected in her 15-blocks-a-day production rate. But this is achieved at the expense of accuracy, from the required +/− 10mm to an actual +/− 15mm. Distracted by other interests, the new manager failed to address Jayne's performance misalignment in much the same way that she failed to address Payne's. And for Jayne, the final misalignment between the organization's revised aspiration to build an arts and performance centre and her personal aspiration to build a cathedral drives her to resign.

So what could the new manager have done differently? You may have your own ideas. Here are a few of mine.

The manager could have started by finding out more about Wayne. She could have spent some quality one-to-one time to find out what makes him tick, what interests him and what may have happened in the past to bring about his current attitude to work. In other words, she could have treated his attitude and behaviours as a symptom of some earlier, as yet unknown, set of causes.

The manager's task with Payne was to assist him in reframing his view of what it means to be a master stonemason in the 21st century, which isn't simply about doing the 'perfect job', regardless of financial cost and environmental impact. The 21st-century stonemason is required to engage with new materials, new methods and new economic realities. If the new manager had inspired Payne to write an article for *The Master Stonemason's Times* detailing the adoption of new construction methods by the Sagrada Familia construction team, she might have achieved her task of engaging Payne with the new realities.

The manager simply needed to be a little more communicative with Sayne. Although he appeared to be personally aligned with his job, stifling his interest in why decisions were being made may ultimately lead to disenchantment – and maybe the development of a new Wayne!

And finally to Jayne. If the new manager had taken the time and care to explain the concept of supporting the crumbling parish churches of Barcelona with the proceeds of the new Gaudi Arts and Performance Centre, and perhaps seeded the thought that Jayne may wish to sit on the GAP Centre Committee in her retirement and contribute to decisions about how the money was spent in future years, she may have aligned Jayne's aspirations with the revised vision for the Sagrada Familia. All a little too straightforward, maybe, but the principles are sound.

Two to three hours will be needed for this exercise.

1. Bring your team members together and ask them to imagine the best possible situation for their team in two years' time. Allow a few minutes for this free flow of thoughts.

2. Place five sheets of flipchart paper around the walls, each with one of the questions below as its header.

    *   Who will be our stakeholders in two years' time?
    *   What will we be doing for them?
    *   How will we want them to see us?
    *   What will make us special?
    *   What will it feel like to work in our team?

3. Ask team members to write their responses to each of these questions on post-it notes and stick them to the appropriate sheet on the wall. They can each produce more than one post-it per sheet – indeed, encourage them to do so.

4. When everyone has run out of ideas, allocate a sheet to each individual (if five or fewer team members are taking part) or to small groups (if six or more are taking part). Ask them to review the post-its and develop a comprehensive and ordered summary on the appropriate flipchart sheet.

5. These summaries can then be fed back to the full group and discussed. Following each discussion, note any goals the team agree to work towards in relation to each sheet. Once all sheets have been covered, stand back and draw out themes and priorities.

6. If time permits, carry out a team coaching exercise on one or more of the priority goals (see Coach). If time is short, return as a group in the near future and carry out the coaching exercise. Alternatively, small groups may take one or two goals each, and return a week or so later with the results of their coaching exercise.

7. Meet with each team member on a one-to-one basis and discuss the session with them. Explore the degree to which the outcomes align with their personal aspirations. Ask them to identify the special contributions they wish to make and follow up any themes in future team meetings and one-to-one sessions.

 To expand on some of the ideas discussed here, see Coach, Involve, Motivation, Unique and Vision.

B

We need to maintain a **balance** of perspectives when assessing how well the business is doing.

Balance

Balance *n.* Harmony in the weighing of factors to create a meaningful whole.

A key component for a fulfilling and successful life is balance. Typically, this is presented to us with the phrase 'work–life balance', and there are many self-help guides available to us if we feel the need for some help in this regard. My own experience of maintaining balance is that the factors I've wished and needed to balance have changed as my career and personal life have evolved. In the early days, I aimed to achieve a balance between sport, an energetic social life and developing my career. Later, priorities changed and career, personal development and travel were centre stage. Now I balance family time, fee-earning work, personal fitness and professional development projects. In essence, my balancing task reflects an evolving set of diverse but interconnected aspirations. And at times of significant transition in my life (e.g. changes of career path, personal relationships and starting a family) I have had to pay particular attention to the balancing act. When I don't get it right I find myself coping with all manner of symptoms and stresses.

No less than for us as complex individuals, so it is that managers and leaders need to consider balance within the context of an evolving set of organizational aspirations, market forces, social changes and economic realities. Essentially, in our organizational roles we need to maintain a balance of perspective when assessing how well the business or service is doing. A tool called the balanced scorecard has proven to be a valuable device for exploring diverse perspectives on performance. Developed by Robert S. Kaplan and David P. Norton (1993), the model facilitates a useful analysis of how an organization is performing relative to its mission. This analysis engages in four key perspectives – Finance, Customer, Internal Processes, and Learning and Growth. As a strategic management tool, the balanced scorecard aligns financial, non-financial, quantitative and qualitative performance measures into a view-at-a-glance framework.

Traditional performance measures that focus on just the financial and operational outcomes of an organization's past are balanced with, and connected to, forward-looking performance indicators linked to less tangible factors such as process innovations, new capabilities and customer relationships. This balance of considerations has the potential to greatly enhance the future and current value of a team or organization.

However, in practice, many balanced scorecards are developed with great promises of what they will do for the organization, but then fail to deliver. Typically this is because the leadership of the organization doesn't effectively communicate strategies to all employees and then help them turn the statements of strategy into statements of local action. My experience suggests that few managers feel confident about soliciting the kind of staff feedback that can fuel innovation at the grass-roots level because it can sound critical or accusatory. The experiences of Kaplan and Norton led them to develop five essential principles for creating and maintaining a balanced, strategy-focused organization:

- Make strategy everyone's job

- Translate your statements of strategy into statements of action

- Align the whole organization to its strategy

- Make change happen through effective leadership

- Continuously review and renew your strategy.

These principles will be further explored in the team exercise that follows later.

A review of the Sagrada Familia story suggests that, with regard to the balanced scorecard, the manager fared reasonably well.

Financial perspective: The manager took account of the financial issues associated with maintaining a building of such great magnitude as the Sagrada Familia. She had witnessed first hand the effect of having inadequate finance to maintain great buildings – in both her holiday destination of Tunbridge Wells and the city of Barcelona, where underfunded parish churches were crumbling. She presented a financial model to the Board of Trustees for the Gaudi Arts and Performance Centre which was comprehensive and grounded in considerations of local demographic change and global tourism. The financial model was also aligned with the project's core values: 25 per cent of profits were to be made available for parish church maintenance across the city.

Customer perspective: Likewise, the new manager engaged with the broad base of customers associated with the building project. Taking Antoni Gaudi as the first customer, she argued the case with respect to his core values, modernist tendencies and consideration of the indigenous religious population of Barcelona. To repeat a critical point, some of the monies generated by the Gaudi Arts and Performance Centre would contribute to the continued maintenance of the parish churches towards which another customer, the local church-going population, had expressed such loyalty. Another group of customers, the broader secular population of Barcelona, would benefit from a world-class venue for the arts, right in the centre of their city. For the business folk of Barcelona, the added attraction of the arts and performance centre would provide further business opportunities through increased levels of cultural tourism.

Internal Processes perspective: Here the new manager did not do so well. For example, consider the operational change from wooden to plastic mallets. Though financially and ecologically sound in principle, the decision was not implemented appropriately. Her management of the transition process was dysfunctional, largely because team members were not involved effectively and little buy-in was achieved. Her management of each individual team member's performance was, likewise, far from balanced. As the stonemasons' performance data presented in the story shows, individual interests rather than the requirements of the job were dominating output.

Learning and Growth perspective: The manager's performance was mixed here. There was no focus in evidence regarding the training and development of the stonemasons, i.e. developing their capabilities to achieve what the organization required of them both now and in the future. Regarding operational and strategic innovations, such as the new mallet and the change of use from cathedral to arts and performance centre, the manager performed well – in principle at least. The shortfall here was in the execution as some key stakeholders were not involved or kept on board. And maybe the extrapolation of the case associated with a parish church in Tunbridge Wells was not fully appropriate to the case of a cathedral in Barcelona. We'll explore this in more detail elsewhere (see Scenario).

 It is best to develop a balanced scorecard for your team with as much participation as possible from those who will be expected to achieve the measures that are established. But prior to the involvement of your team it may be helpful to work through the following steps on your own (or with a colleague) in order to better understand the concept and get a feel for what a balanced scorecard would look like for your team. You'll then be better prepared to include your team in the process.

1. Beginning with the team's vision and mission statements, brainstorm the key measures that might be included under each of the scorecard's four perspectives. See Figure 3 for some examples.

2. Having generated as wide a range of measures as possible, rank-order them in terms of their ease of measurement and the degree to which they truly indicate how well you are doing in achieving your mission.

3. Select the key measures you will work with, but don't discard the others. They may be revisited in the light of experience.

4. Where possible, establish current performance levels against each of the chosen key measures. Estimate if necessary.

5. Agree targets for future performance against each measure.

6.   Develop action plans to achieve the targeted performance.

7.   Establish systems to collect ongoing performance data.

8.   Review and act upon the performance data.

9.   At least annually, revisit your scorecard to see how well it's serving you.

10. In the light of the review, change or modify your scorecard.

	Last year's performance	Next year's target	Target for three years
Financial perspective			
Operating income			
Return on capital employed			
Unit costs of performing work			
Customer perspective			
Customer satisfaction			
Customer retention			
New customer acquisition			
Internal Process perspective			
Strategic and business planning			
Introduction of innovations			
Efficiency improvements			
Learning and Growth perspective			
Employee satisfaction			
Multi/new-skills development			
Staff retention			

Figure 3: Template for a balanced scorecard

To expand on some of the ideas discussed here, see Aspiration, Involve, Motivation, Scenario, Transition and Vision.

C

Surprisingly good things can happen with individuals and teams if they are supported by a manager's efforts and the application of the **coach**ing process.

Coach

Coach *vb.* To facilitate an improvement in performance by questioning, challenging and supporting.

During the early part of my career I was privileged to work with a senior manager who had an outstanding ability to ask pertinent questions and then listen patiently to me as I worked towards meaningful answers. I never felt directed towards a particular outcome or plan of action. Indeed, I don't know if Mike, the senior manager in question, ever had his own specific thoughts on the issues we explored. But he always created the conditions within which I was able to develop well-considered and confident action plans. So it was that I experienced, as recipient, the empowering benefits of good coaching practice. Thereafter, and within my various roles as manager and leader, coaching became a valued means of assessing and improving the performance of both individuals and teams. I have experienced, as a coaching-style manager, how the process has helped others deepen their learning, improve their performance and enhance their quality of life. In designated coaching meetings I learned to listen, contribute my observations and ask well-selected questions. Through this process the individuals and teams I've worked with have created clarity of purpose, moved towards effective action and accelerated their development and performance. I have further learned that it is critical to understand where teams and individuals are in the here-and-now and to appreciate what they're willing to do to get to where they want to be in the future. The coaching process recognizes that results are a matter of intentions, choices and actions. I have found almost without exception that surprisingly good things can happen with individuals and teams if they are supported by a manager's efforts and the application of the coaching process.

There is much confusion about what coaching is, as compared with counselling, consulting and mentoring. Here are some common examples used within the coaching community to explain the differences. If you wished to learn how to ride a bicycle and hired a:

- *Counsellor:* The counsellor would help you discover what is holding you back from riding the bicycle. They would go back into your past to discover what kind of experience you had at an early age with a bicycle.

- *Consultant:* The consultant would bring you a bicycle manual and tell you everything you ever wanted to know about the workings of a bicycle. The consultant would then depart and return six months later to see how you were doing.

- *Mentor:* The mentor would share their experiences of bicycle riding and the lessons they had learned. The mentor would bestow all their bicycle-related wisdom onto you.

- *Coach:* The coach would help you get up on the bicycle and then encourage, endorse, acknowledge and support you while running alongside until you felt comfortable enough to go it alone. They might then return every so often to help you become excellent at riding a bicycle.

An approach to coaching that has been successfully adopted by many managers and professional coaches over the past two decades utilizes the GROW model, an acronym of Goal/Reality/Options/Will.

Goal   Reality   Options   Will

This model provides a simple yet powerful framework for structuring a coaching session. A useful metaphor for the GROW model is the way you might coach a team member who was about to undertake an important (bicycle) journey. First, and with the aid of an appropriate map, you would help your team member decide where they are going (their Goal) and where they are now (their Reality). Then you would explore various ways of making the journey (the Options). In the final step of the process (establishing the Will) you would ensure your team member was committed to making the journey and was prepared for the conditions and obstacles they might meet along the way.

Continuing this illustration into workplace practice, the GROW framework consists of the following four steps:

Step 1: Goal. The manager and team member establish a specific goal for the discussion. This goal should be within the span of control or influence of the team member, i.e. it needs to be something the team member can realistically achieve. Thereafter, manager and team member agree on a number of clear measures that will indicate the goal has been achieved.

Step 2: Reality. Both manager and team member explore the current situation with regard to what is 'real' at present and the associated consequences of this reality. The aim here is to achieve the most accurate picture possible of what is currently going on.

Step 3: Options. During the options stage the manager's aim is to draw out a list of all possible actions the team member might take – without judgement or evaluation. The manager draws out suggestions from the team member by asking effective questions and then guiding them towards making the most appropriate choice(s) through a cost–benefit analysis.

Step 4: Will. The manager's aim during this stage is to gain commitment to action. The manager and team member agree the most appropriate choices for action, commit to their individual and collective contributions, draw up an action plan and identify how to overcome potential obstacles.

There were numerous opportunities for the manager to engage with coaching sessions with her staff in our opening story.

For example, regarding Wayne's sickness absence record, on Wayne's return to work following the first bout of 'sickness' a coaching session around the goal of 'improving Wayne's attendance' would almost certainly have made a significant inroad into this issue. The appropriate map would be the *organization's guidelines on sickness absence and its management*. The goal would be *to reduce Wayne's absence*. The current situation would be *the record of Wayne's absence* and *associated observations*, i.e. absence has tended to follow the introduction of a change in working routine. Options to be generated might include:

- A programme of further coaching to explore the underlying issues associated with Wayne's general attitude to work

- Additional support from the manager when communicating change

- Buddying up with a colleague who works positively with change

- A training course on 'Managing change and transitions'

- A visit to the organization's occupational health adviser

- Finally, and as a last resort (when other options have failed to deliver within a reasonable time frame), formal capability or disciplinary action.

These options could be explored with Wayne to establish the way forward. Thereafter, individual responsibilities could be agreed and plans put in place to review progress.

Likewise, with Payne and Jayne, their attitudes towards new mallets and art centres could have been explored. Respectively, the maps would be *improving cost-effectiveness using environmentally sustainable methods* and *creating a building that is fit for 21st-century purpose.* By way of an exercise you might put yourself in Payne's or Jayne's position and work through the 18 coaching questions provided below. Depending on the stance you adopt, the result will be either a planned withdrawal from the organization or a renewed commitment to the organization based on a new mindset. Either result would, most likely, be preferable to the resentful withdrawal described in our story.

The manager's interactions with Sayne presented the most straightforward opportunities to engage in coaching, but none were taken. Significantly, Sayne's high level of independence in his job, linked to the quality and quantity of his output, may have seduced the manager into thinking he required little maintenance. However, all staff need maintenance if they are to become and remain fit for purpose! This is a concept we'll explore elsewhere (see Lead).

Clearly, coaching would have made a significant demand on the manager's time. This must be weighed against the time taken in dealing with the consequences of *not* coaching her staff.

While some managers are fortunate enough to get formal training as coaches, most are not. For the majority, if they wish to develop coaching skills they have to do it for themselves. The following exercise is aimed at helping you to develop as a coach with the assistance of friends, colleagues, individual team members and your team as a whole.

There are four steps to this exercise, any of which can be repeated any number of times:

Step 1: Coach a friend.

Step 2: Coach a work colleague.

Step 3: Coach a team member.

Step 4: Coach your team or a section of your team.

As you enter into each of these situations you can use the questions provided below to prompt you through the coaching process.

Goal

1. With regard to a current challenge or outstanding issue, what do you want to achieve?

2. How will you measure your success (at least three tangible measures)?

3. When do you want to achieve it by (specific date)?

Reality

4. What is the current situation (what, when, how)?

5. What have you done so far?

6. What results did that produce?

7. What's holding you back?

8. What do you have that you're not using?

Options

9. What options do you have (list at least three then add 'do nothing')?

10. What are the benefits and costs of each (including the 'do nothing' option)?

11. What else could you do (stretch yourself to come up with a further option)?

12. What are the benefits and costs of the additional option?

Will

13. Which option or options do you choose?

14. What could arise to hinder you?

15. What will you do to overcome these hindrances?

16. What help do you need and from whom?

17. Who needs to know what you're doing/planning?

18. What are you going to do now (i.e. create an action plan)?

When working with friends, colleagues or team members, it is important that you say why you are doing the exercise, i.e. to develop your coaching skills. This will create a tolerance of the relatively rigid initial approach and enable you to ask for and receive honest feedback from your coachees regarding how useful they found the exercise. As you gain more experience and confidence, you will develop a more personal style. But in the early stages of your practice, I believe you would be wise to stick as closely as possible to the format and questions suggested above.

Finally, you might find it useful to keep a diary/learning log to note your reflections as you gain more experience in coaching. This will accelerate and deepen the learning process.

 To expand on some of the ideas discussed here, see also Kaizen, Lead, Motivation, Question and Relationship.

D

We must exploit new opportunities to **delegate** as a matter of routine.

Delegate

Delegate *vb*. To give tasks, responsibilities, accountabilities, etc. to another person.

Delegation has made a highly significant contribution to my personal and professional development from two perspectives. As my corporate career evolved, tasks and responsibilities delegated to me provided challenge and gave me a growing sense of progress. This said, a landmark event in my development arose from a misunderstanding. I'd been working in Shell's strategic planning function for around three months and one of my senior colleagues was preparing to deliver the Scenario Planning contribution at Shell's Graduate Orientation Course (GOC), a sort of super induction programme that took place over a five-week period in the Netherlands. I had never been on one of these courses as a participant and expressed an interest in attending. This request was heard as me wishing to present the Scenario Planning contribution. This misunderstanding only became clear to me when, two weeks later, a colleague placed the Scenario Planning file in my hand and said I was to present on the next programme, a month later. I could have corrected the misunderstanding but chose instead to accept the challenge. And it was a challenge – but I survived. In fact, following my delivery of the materials I had been given I redesigned the Scenario Planning contribution. Instead of it being a relatively dry PowerPoint presentation over three hours, I negotiated with the GOC course managers that we would have a full day that included scenario and option planning exercises that would give participants a hands-on experience of how Shell carried out its strategic planning. I went on to deliver the new programme half a dozen times with great success. Delegation, during the early stages of my career, and whether planned or misunderstood, proved to be an excellent stimulus to my development – both professionally and personally.

Turning to my experiences of delegation from the other side of the process, on later becoming a team leader within Shell Ventures, I had to come to terms with the discomfort I felt when delegating tasks and responsibilities to others. Overcoming this discomfort marked my true transition into the leadership role. It was through my early attempts at delegation that I came to discover the quality of my communications and the nature of my professional anxieties. Regarding communication, I learned to be clear and uncluttered in what I requested from people – particularly with regard to deadlines and measurable outcomes. In terms of my anxieties as a professional, I learned how overly attached I was to doing the perfect job in my own, 'right' way. As I gained experience and confidence in the leadership role I became more trusting of my staff to do what was required in *their* particular way. I also became more understanding of my role in developing people such that they were supported in taking on more tasks and greater responsibilities without feeling either micro-managed or abandoned.

Given the time and performance pressures placed on most of us in today's hectic work environment, it is crucial that we concentrate our time on activities that nobody else can do, such as planning, appraising and developing staff, managing team priorities and performance, recruiting and integrating new members of the team and facilitating effective teamworking. In order to have the time to do this, we must exploit new opportunities to delegate as a matter of routine. And if we see delegation as a two-dimensional task, the first dimension being aimed at our own effective use of time and the second dimension being aimed at developing our staff and our team, we have a dual incentive to make delegation work effectively and to the fullest possible extent.

Of course, as a responsible manager it is important to look out for signs that we are overloading staff.

As will be explored in greater detail elsewhere (see Lead), delegation is one of four styles of leadership and forms part of a natural progression from directing to coaching, mentoring and, ultimately, delegating. Furthermore, delegation is a deeply misunderstood concept. Phrases often associated with delegation include:

- I don't have the time to show her how to do it

- It's quicker to do it myself

- I could do it better myself

- I don't know if I can trust him to do it

- She isn't qualified to do it

- He doesn't want any added responsibilities

- She already has enough to do

- I'm the only person who knows how to do this

- I don't want to give up this task because I like doing it.

We use many excuses for not delegating tasks and responsibilities. Often our reasons are unfounded. What delegation is actually about is *developing* people. If we assume the opposite of the above statements is true, we may be surprised by what people can and will do.

There were no examples of delegation in practice within our opening scenario. Ironically, the appropriate use of delegation may have brought about improved motivation and performance in at least three of the stonemasons. To reiterate a critical point made earlier, delegation is about *developing* people. So how might this particular team of stonemasons have been developed? The full answer is 'in many ways!'

As ever, Wayne remains the special case in our scenario – we still have to discover what makes him tick. Maybe the timely procurement of raw materials (piles of rocks) could be delegated to him. His performance issue was sickness absence and this was apparently related, in one instance, to the stress associated with the delivery of rocks. In Wayne's own words, 'When that pile over there is just about used up, a truck comes round the corner and dumps a whole pile more.' If we accept this on face value as the real problem for Wayne (but there are clear indications we should not) we might explore the feasibility of deliveries being scheduled in such a way as to create a smoother workflow instead of the current situation which is one of being presented with an overwhelming quantity of work – just when things seemed to be getting under control. Wayne might be delegated the task of investigating this possibility.

Payne's performance issue was an exaggerated emphasis on quality at the expense of meeting his quantitative production target. In addition he had a problem with the adoption of new-style mallets which he refused to accept could be fit for purpose. Often, when I have presented this scenario on leadership programmes, participants will initially suggest that Payne be delegated the task of evaluating the new mallet on behalf of the project and his fellow stonemasons. However, on further reflection participants conclude that this should be avoided given that Payne's very identity as a master stonemason is tied up in the use of his traditional wooden mallet. It is highly unlikely that Payne will engage in an objective evaluation of the new mallet's merits or suitability for the job in hand given this issue of identity. More appropriately, Payne might be delegated the task of drawing up a quantity/quality matrix for the production of blocks using the old and the new mallets. Essentially, this could involve an incremental study in which Payne determined how many blocks he and his colleagues could produce per day using the old and new mallets and by adopting different tolerances of accuracy. A delegated study such as this may:

(a)   Help engage Wayne as he would be drawn into a team effort that highlighted his consistent on-target performance with regard to the quality and quantity of building blocks

(b)   Improve Jayne's performance by enabling her to appreciate the negative effect of her focus on quantity at the expense of quality

(c)   Improve Payne's performance by enabling him to appreciate the negative effect of his focus on quality. It may also 'correct' for any biases Payne has against the new mallet by highlighting his performance in comparison to that of Jayne, Sayne and Wayne when using the new mallet.

Sayne's response to all incidents of change (i.e. new mallets and new strategic direction) was one of healthy interest and measured consideration. For me, this indicates that he may have management potential. The manager might have started to explore options for further developing Sayne in this direction.

Regarding Jayne, if she had been delegated some of the tasks involved in establishing the business case that explored the potential strengths and weaknesses of building a cathedral as opposed to an arts and performance centre in 21st-century Barcelona, her commitment to continue working on the project in the light of the strategic change might have been maintained.

Finally, we might also delegate to Wayne, Payne, Sayne and Jayne the task of continuous improvement in all things (see Kaizen for more).

The activity that follows will help you answer the question 'How might I expand on my current levels of delegation?'

1.   Complete the template illustrated in Figure 4 for each member of your team.

2.   Taking your comments from the right-hand column, i.e. additional activities/responsibilities that could be delegated, draw up a draft plan for delegating the identified activities for each team member.

3.   Meet with each team member and discuss your thoughts and plans.

4.   Be specific about the outcomes you wish to achieve and listen carefully to their comments, concerns and further suggestions.

5.   If/when the delegated tasks or responsibilities are transferred, be sure to maintain the appropriate balance between ensuring the person is supported while letting go and allowing them to complete the job and learn from their experience. Adopting a coaching style of support may be appropriate (see Coach).

6.   Reward successful performance (and success should be inevitable if steps 1 to 5 above have been followed).

Team member's name	Current activities/ responsibilities delegated	Additional activities/ responsibilities that could be delegated
Routine activities		
Fact finding		
Problem analysis and option generation		
Wider contribution		

Figure 4: Template for delegation planning

 To expand on some of the ideas discussed here, see Coach, Kaizen, Lead, Motivation and Question.

E

By exploring **external** trends, we can begin to understand, anticipate and prepare for the future.

External

External *adj.* Situated on, or acting from, the outside.

When things go well (e.g. we win a race, pass an exam or achieve a good outcome from a project), people will congratulate us. If we're modest we'll say something like 'Oh, I had a good start', or 'The right questions came up', or 'It was the rest of the team really'. This modesty may of course benefit us when things don't go so well because then we can say 'Oh, I had a really bad start' or 'All the wrong questions came up' or 'It was the rest of the team's fault really'. If we're less modest, we'll take credit for our achievements but be less well positioned when things don't work out so well. In truth, outcomes are a combination of the actions we take within complex environments. The better we understand ourselves and our environments the better will be the consequences of our actions – probably!

In my experience of family life, best-practice decision making takes place around the dinner table when we spontaneously explore 'what if' statements and play out scenarios. Scenarios will be explored in depth in a dedicated section later, but here we'll prepare for that exploration by focusing on the external environments we populate in our everyday and organizational lives. These external environments are characterized by variables such as trends in society, the price of things, what others close to us are doing and what the media say. In our personal lives all of these factors apply whether we are talking about our next holiday, moving house, making a choice of schools for our children, or deciding what to do with our investments. The often uncomfortable truth is that no one can predict what the future will bring with any meaningful accuracy. But by exploring external trends we can begin to understand, anticipate and prepare for the future.

One method that is widely used to look at external trends is STEEPLE analysis. This identifies some of the key external issues that exist (or are emerging) and suggests how these might impact on the future strategy, operations and resources of the organization. And the mnemonic 'STEEPLE' provides a useful memory aid for ordering our thinking across a range of external factors.

My preferred range of STEEPLE factors (other sources will vary) is as follows:

- Socio-cultural factors – e.g. population demographics, lifestyle changes, levels of education, people's attitudes to work and leisure, income distribution

- Technological factors – e.g. new discoveries/developments, speed of technology transfer, industry's focus on technological effort, government spending on research

- Economic factors – e.g. interest rates, inflation, unemployment, levels of disposable income, business cycles, GNP trends

- Environmental factors – e.g. local authority environmental policies, environmental protection laws, the activities of pressure groups

- Political factors – e.g. the stability of the government, foreign trade regulations, other regulation and deregulation trends, taxation policy

- Legal factors – e.g. monopolies legislation, employment laws, discrimination laws

- E-business factors – e.g. buying and selling through the internet, web-enabled multimedia conferencing, increases in remote working, on-line marketing.

As a starting point for the analysis, each STEEPLE factor is addressed in turn and trends that may affect the business over the next few years are brainstormed. Then, having produced what is probably quite a long list, the next step is to look at each of the trends and ask, 'How can we accommodate or control this?'

Having looked at potential future trends through STEEPLE analysis, leaders and planners can incorporate the outputs into strategic development, operational planning and continuous improvement initiatives. Those who do this well have the best chance of maintaining their competitive edge.

Our construction manager appeared to have a reasonable grasp of STEEPLE analysis. Her awareness of new materials prompted an operational change in the type of mallets used on the project and her experiences in Tunbridge Wells prompted a change in strategic direction. The manager's version of a STEEPLE analysis may have looked something like the illustration in Figure 5.

A further analysis in one or two years' time will almost certainly reveal different trends. Furthermore, a STEEPLE analysis is only as good as the data and knowledge that are invested in the process. For example, if the construction manager had visited some of the great British cathedrals she would have seen that some of these, in response to social–cultural trends, effectively combine performance, concert and faith activities in one venue, creating a rich resource for the wider communities in which they are placed. York Minster offers an excellent case in point which may have provided a more appropriate strategic benchmark than a converted parish church in Tunbridge Wells.

Environmental factors	Trends/issues	Potential impact on the building project and options for organizational response
Socio-cultural	Growth in secular proportion of the population; expansion of cultural tourism	Establish a world-class arts and performance centre to attract cultural tourists to Barcelona
Technological	Developments in materials technologies	Seek opportunities to exploit developments such as computer-aided design technologies to test revised structural plans
Economic	Increased levels of disposable income in the developing world	Attract financial sponsors to the arts and performance centre with offers such as life membership benefits
Environmental	Drive towards the green agenda and reducing carbon footprints	Introduce environmentally sound construction methods, e.g. mallets made from recycled materials
Political	Governmental policy for the development of transport infrastructure	With plans being progressed to build a tunnel associated with a high-speed rail link beneath cathedral foundations, establish an influential lobby to challenge local policy
Legal	Lack or response from city council to two planning requests (in 1916 and 1990)	Seek clarification of city council's position and if necessary engage legal assistance to challenge delays in responses
E-business	Growth in the development and use of internet-mediated activities and services	Promote the arts and performance centre via the internet, e.g. virtual tours of the facilities and webcasts of performance events

Figure 5: STEEPLE analysis – the Gaudi scenario

Building on the final point made above, i.e. given that the quality of the output from a STEEPLE analysis is highly dependent on the quality of the input, it is best to carry out the analysis for your organization with as many knowledgeable participants as possible. External experts are often engaged in such analyses. However, we will concentrate on an internal team analysis and three to four hours will be required for the following exercise.

1. If more than six people are participating in the exercise, divide the group into subgroups of between three and five members. Each group can work on the following tasks independently and all group outputs can be collated and synthesized in the final session.

2. As a starting point, look at each of the STEEPLE factors in turn and brainstorm those that you believe might affect your organization over the next few years. The template and descriptions provided earlier may help in this task, but only complete the first column at this stage.

3. Having produced your list, look at each of the trends identified and ask yourselves:

    (a) How might this affect us?
    (b) How might we reduce potential negative effects on us?
    (c) How might we exploit this trend as an opportunity?

    Your output from these considerations can be placed in the second column.

4. If more than one group is working on this exercise, bring the groups together to share and combine their various outputs.

5. Taking the output from step 3, and while still in the full group, develop a series of goals associated with defending against potential threats and exploiting potential opportunities.

6. Allocate subgroups to a selection of these goals and carry out a series of coaching exercises to establish possible paths forward (see Coach).

To expand on some of the ideas discussed here, see Balance, Coach, Option, Scenario and Unique.

F

 If the **force** resisting change is stronger than that driving change, much effort will be expended on change not happening.

Force

Force *n*. Energy that is applied to an object or a person in order to bring about movement or change.

 I sometimes amaze myself! There are perfectly good reasons why I should do something (improve my fitness, settle down to a work task, decorate the bathroom) but I don't get around to it. My family and friends may prompt me and reinforce the good reasons over and over again, but I still don't get on with it. What's going on? Well, from the standpoint of simple logic, the pay-off I feel from not doing something is greater than the pay-off I think I'll get from doing it. Working with this simple logic, and engaging in some honest reflections, I am able to see, almost without exception, what's stopping me. Current resistances are fuelled by thoughts like 'jogging around the streets is boring and I'm not that unfit' – but the truth is I'm being lazy! When not settling to a work task, my internal voice tells me I'll be in a better frame of mind to write that report after I've got lots of other fiddly little jobs out of the way – but the truth is I know this is going to be a difficult report to write and I don't yet feel up to the challenge. Regarding the bathroom, I tell myself that decorating is best done in the spring/summer/autumn/winter (with deletions as appropriate to suit the current season) but the truth is that I think the bathroom looks fine and there are lots of other things I'd rather do – like strumming my guitar for a few hours. Reflecting on and addressing these resistances is the key to progress and always brings me a better outcome than having others repeatedly reinforcing the 'good reasons' or 'drivers' for why I should do something. Herein lies the key message of force field analysis.

Kurt Lewin, thought by some to be the founder of social psychology, developed his ideas around force field analysis in the 1950s (Lewin, 1951). Since then his model has become one of the most influential developments in the field of social science and organization development. Force field analysis provides a framework for looking at the factors (forces) that influence a situation. It distinguishes between forces that are either driving movement towards a goal (drivers) or blocking movement towards a goal (resistors). When used in its typical form, force field analysis provides a visual representation of the factors that aid and hinder a targeted change. The process of carrying out a force field analysis can make a significant contribution to action planning for change as the act of asking people about their concerns (resistances) regarding a targeted change is a key part of involvement and consultation. In simple terms, if the force resisting change is stronger than that driving change, much effort will be expended on change not happening.

Resistance is common to all situations that focus on changing the processes and/or structures within an organization. The leader who wishes to implement change needs a well-developed ability to recognize and address the forces that are resistant to change. And in order to understand resistance it is important to keep in mind that the way an organization is structured and operates is down to someone or some group somewhere having taken the decision that this is the way it should be. So change, particularly for them, can be highly threatening.

Furthermore, resistance can be direct or indirect. Direct resistance is characterized by an authentic (uncluttered, honest and open) response to a perceived threat, combined with an open expression of why change is being resisted. Indirect resistance is characterized by a lack of authenticity and a silent/masked withdrawal of co-operation. Usually resistance is indirect and, consequently, difficult for us to address effectively. However, Peter Block (2000) provides us with some clear advice about how to recognize and deal with resistance.

Typical indicators of indirect resistance include:

- Not answering the phone or emails

- Not turning up for team meetings or one-to-ones

- Not preparing adequately for meetings or one-to-ones

- Continuing to question the same piece of information or instruction, even after it has been repeated several times

- Appearing irritable

- Responding to requests for information or help in an untimely manner

- Being quiet and/or uncommunicative

- Overly intellectualizing

- Poor timekeeping and increased sickness absence.

Suggested steps for dealing with resistance are:

- Recognizing it – by recognizing the typical indicators (see above)

- Acknowledging it – by naming the behaviours you are seeing in simple, specific and brief terms

- Further acknowledging it by then letting people have their say without fear of being judged

- Not taking it personally – what people are (probably) resisting is change, not you

- Exploring ways forward – initially, by asking those who are resisting what they want to do about the situation, as this helps them take responsibility for their thoughts and feelings

- Focusing on agreements – as even modest agreements represent a win–win situation.

In our opening story, Wayne's resistance to all forms of change was indirect, and predictable. He simply took sick leave!

Payne's resistance to the operational change in the use of mallets was, in the first instance, both direct and authentic. He made clear his objections and the reasons behind them, i.e. the new mallets would not allow him to maintain his identity as a master stonemason of three generations' standing. One might reasonably expect that, following the failure of the manager to engage effectively with Payne's direct resistance, he would then have engaged in indirect resistance. This may have taken the form of stirring up trouble with his master stonemason colleagues and continuing to use his traditional mallet whenever he felt he would get away with it. This said, Payne reverted to the most sincere and extreme form of resistance in the final reckoning – he resigned from his job.

Sayne showed no overt signs of either direct or indirect resistance. He simply requested more information in order that he might understand and judge for himself the validity of the changes that were being imposed. This analysis of Sayne's behaviour does, however, raise the question of how long he might absorb the manager's lack of engagement with his own healthy curiosity.

Jayne was initially more subtle in her resistance to the strategic change (i.e. from building a cathedral to building an arts and performance centre). She became quiet and uncommunicative. But then, two weeks later, like Payne she expressed the ultimate resistance by resigning from her job.

Had the manager engaged with Payne's direct resistance and Jayne's indirect resistance at the point of its first expression (see Aspiration for an example of how she might have achieved this), these pinches may have been prevented from becoming crunches (see Relationship for more on pinches and crunches).

In the exercise that follows you are invited to explore with your team a change situation that is real and current for you. As with other exercises, you may wish to complete this exercise on your own first to better understand and adapt the process to your own team context.

1.	Bring your team together and, following an appropriate introduction, use a flipchart page to note the change to be explored. Display this at one end of a clear expanse of wall.

2.	On a second sheet, state clearly the current situation and place this sheet beneath the first (see Figure 6).

3.	Ask team members to write their thoughts on the advantages and disadvantages of maintaining the status quo on post-it notes. Encourage them to write as many responses as they can. These should be attached to the second sheet.

4.	Group together and summarize the posted notes from step 3.

5.	State clearly the desired situation on a third flipchart sheet and, as with step 3, ask team members to post their thoughts on the advantages and disadvantages associated with the desired situation.

6.	Group together and summarize the posted notes from step 5.

7.	Build the case for change on a fourth flipchart sheet using all of the information elicited from steps 1 to 6.

8.	On a fifth flipchart sheet, list a range of options for action that will move you from the current situation to the desired situation.

9.	Analyse the options to determine the best options.

10.	Build an action plan for the favoured option.

11.	Brainstorm resistors to the change and its associated action plan.

12.	Develop an understanding of the causal factors that lie beneath the resistors and add further actions to your action plan as required to address the resistance issues raised.

Change to be Explored A clear statement here			

The Current Situation (Post-it notes on the advantages and disadvantages of maintaining the status quo)	**The Desired Situation** (Post-it notes on the advantages and disadvantages of the desired situation)	**Options for Actions** A list of options generated by the group here	**Action Plan**

The Case for Change	**Resistors to the Change**

Figure 6: Arranging flipchart sheets for force field analysis

To expand on some of the ideas discussed here, see Aspiration, Coach, Motivation, Relationship and Transition.

G

 Effective **goal** setting is now almost universally recognized as the most powerful way to improve performance.

Goal

Goal *n*. The aim or object to which our efforts are directed. The end point of a journey or race.

 There is a well-worn adage that if you don't know where you're heading, any destination will do. Few of us would accept any destination yet many of us fail to identify unambiguously where we're headed. We've explored the concept of aspiration elsewhere. One of my aspirations in the early 1990s was to become a competent and confident yachtmaster. I'd been sailing with a colleague some ten years earlier and found the experience both exciting and 'spiritual'. But I was nervous about open water. So, I set myself a progressive set of goals as follows:

- Join Whitstable Yacht Club and learn the rudiments of sailing in dinghies

- Complete a Day Skipper Theory course at my local Adult Education Centre

- Complete a Day Skipper Practical course

- Find myself a mentor

- Complete a Yachtmaster Theory course

- Buy a yacht

- Take my Yachtmaster Practical exam on my own yacht

- Enjoy sailing for the rest of my life!

My aspiration was broken down into a series of specific, realistic and timely goals, with each goal representing a significant step on my journey. Crucially, there were three important attributes associated with my set of goals: they were focused on a final outcome that I personally valued, they were each realistic and they contained many feedback opportunities.

I stuck to my goals and had an exciting and enjoyable journey. Gordon was my mentor and for a couple of years we sailed in his yacht. Thereafter, when I bought my own yacht, he helped me prepare for my Yachtmaster Offshore Practical exam. I joined a team that sailed across the North Atlantic and later gained a commercial endorsement. This enabled me to use my yacht for team building and leadership training – far exceeding my original plans and expectations.

Had I not planned my approach, I doubt I would have enjoyed and achieved quite as much.

Edwin A. Locke began to examine his ideas around goal setting in the mid-1960s. His research began by focusing on the impact goal setting has on individual performance and the results of his work (Locke, 1996, 2001), though often perceived as common sense, do contain some surprises. Let's explore!

Goals can affect performance in three ways. First, goals focus attention and direct efforts towards goal-relevant activities and away from goal-irrelevant activities. Second, goals can lead to more effort. For example, if it is comfortable to produce ten widgets an hour and the goal is to produce twelve, people are likely to work more intensely than they otherwise would to reach the goal. For goals to increase performance it is critical that they be challenging because performance tends to be lower with easily attained goals than with more challenging goals. Third, goals promote persistence. People are more likely to work through setbacks if they are pursuing a goal rather than being asked to carry out a task. Beyond these basic points, the goal/performance relationship is subject to a range of *moderators*. Here are three such moderators.

- Goal commitment. This is the most influential moderator. Being personally committed is particularly important with difficult or complex goals. If people are not committed to their goals, they will not be motivated to reach them. And in order for someone to be committed to a goal, they must believe it is important or significant – to them.

- Goal attainability. Individuals must also believe that the goal is attainable. If they think there is no chance of achieving it they may not even try.

- Goal feedback. In order for goals to enhance performance there also needs to be feedback. It is difficult for goals to be effective if an individual cannot check progress in relation to their goal. It is important that people know where they stand in achieving their goal, so they can determine if they need to commit more effort or resources, or if they should change their methods.

If the above ideas do not seem revolutionary, this serves to illustrate the impact that Locke's work has made on professional and personal performance theory over the past forty years. Effective goal setting is now almost universally recognized as the most powerful way to improve performance. Indeed, the value of goal setting is so well recognized that entire management systems such as Management by Objectives (MBO) incorporate all the goal-setting basics within their structure.

Many people will be familiar with the mnemonic 'SMART' in relation to goals. A range of definitions of SMART have evolved since the 1960s. My preferred choice is as follows:

- **Specific** – the goal is stated unambiguously as a single targeted outcome.

- **Measurable** – the goal has at least one but preferably more measures of success.

- **Agreed** – all parties upon whom the goal has an influence or impact are in agreement with the goal. Failure to have all-party agreement will almost certainly end in failure to achieve the goal.

- **Realistic** – the most common reason a goal isn't achieved is because it was unrealistic from the outset. Judgements about what is 'realistic' need to be made with a number of considerations in mind:
  - The degree of challenge, given other goals and responsibilities that need to be met
  - The abilities of those actively responsible for achieving the goal
  - External/environmental issues
  - The alignment of values
  - Reward strategies.

- **Timely** – this means 'of its time', i.e. this is the appropriate time to be pursuing this goal.

A review of the manager's response to goal setting reveals typical weak spots in the goal-setting process (see Figure 7). A glance at the ticks, question marks and crosses marked in the table indicates that weak spots are typically associated with the 'Agreed' and 'Realistic' criteria. Beyond this, a more detailed analysis reveals the subtleties associated with effective goal setting. The examples illustrated in Figure 7 relate to productivity, sickness absence and the ultimate goal of Antoni Gaudi.

Regarding the number of building blocks to be produced each day (productivity), and their acceptable size tolerances (accuracy), Wayne's and Sayne's performance provides evidence that these are realistic goals. Payne and Jayne have placed a different personal emphasis on accuracy and productivity, but their performance still serves to reinforce the idea that the goal as set is realistic. The debate to be engaged in here concerns the feasibility of changing their individual attitudes on what they see as a job well done.

	Audit result against 'SMART'				
Goal as stated	**Specific**	**Measurable**	**Agreed**	**Realistic**	**Timely**
Each day, produce 10 building blocks to within +/– 10mm tolerances of the current working template.	✓ The goal is stated unambiguously as a targeted outcome.	✓ Quantity, quality and timescale are specified.	? Payne and Jayne have agendas that conflict with the measures associated with the goal.	? Wayne's and Saynes's performance indicates that this is realistic – but this is a complex judgement.	✓ This appears to be a reasonable expectation given the production methods – so is 'of its time'.
Take no more than 8 days sickness leave within each calendar year.	✓ The goal is stated unambiguously as a targeted outcome within a specific time frame.	✓ Quantity and timescale are specified.	? For Wayne, there is no agreement with this goal.	✓ Barring accidents and serious illness, this is a realistic goal in the 21st century.	✓ The goal is probably consistent with current recognized HR practice – so is 'of its time'.
To build the finest structure in the Christian world for the people of Barcelona to celebrate their faith.	? Gaudi envisaged the finest structure in the Christian world – completed within no specific time frame.	X There are no clear measures and, in the end, 'finest structure' may be a subjective judgement.	? Only Jayne and one of the trustees held on firmly to the goal as originally stated.	X The goal, as originally stated, was unrealistic for many reasons.	X The manager's trip to Tunbridge Wells suggested the project was no longer 'of its time'.

Figure 7: Auditing objectives against 'SMART' criteria – the Gaudi scenario

Regarding sickness absence, the only question within the opening scenario concerns Wayne's apparent record of injury (repetitive strain injuries). If this sickness absence is genuine, then an investigation into Wayne's methods of working may be the first approach. If no problems are revealed here, the next step would be to look into Wayne's general health. Only after these two avenues of investigation have been exhausted would it be appropriate to investigate potential causes associated with Wayne's attitude to his job.

Regarding Antoni Gaudi's ultimate goal of building the finest structure in the Christian world, this is a subjective and hence unmeasurable goal.

 Here we will explore the goal-setting processes you currently employ.

Bearing in mind the SMART guidelines outlined earlier, this exercise will focus on the goals that are current for your team. You may find it useful to create a matrix similar to that outlined in Figure 7.

1.	Select three individual or team goals and write them down as they are currently stated.

2.	Apply the SMART test systematically, i.e. for each component of SMART, carry out an audit on each of your stated objectives. Be critical!

3.	Revise or modify the three stated goals as appropriate in the light of the results of your audit.

4.	This exercise can be repeated with members of your team either within a one-to-one meeting or as part of a team development exercise.

5.	In all future goal-setting activities, apply the SMART criteria before finally formalizing goals.

To expand on some of the ideas discussed here, see Aspiration, Coaching, Question, Relationship and Vision.

H

 We don't have to function on 'autopilot' even though we often do, out of **habit**.

Habit

Habit *n*. A tendency to act in a particular way. A learned behavioural response to a particular situation.

 I am a creature of numerous and diverse habits. I shower and clean my teeth a couple of times a day; I say 'please' and 'thank you' in response to requests and receipts; I stay up late and eat toast at around midnight; I respond to over 90 per cent of my emails immediately on opening them; I leave 'preparation' until the last minute; I overcommit myself and then get stressed when I'm overcommitted. As I reflect on my habits I get the uncomfortable feeling that virtually everything I do is habitual! Some of these habits are highly functional, others less so. But regardless of how functional they are, they are all difficult to change. And it probably goes without saying that the longer I've clung to my habits (some since my early childhood) the harder they are to break or, more appropriately, replace.

Stephen Covey (1989) details an approach to personal change and development that focuses on habits he believes will bring us greater success. The first three habits explored by Covey deal with personal development.

1. Be proactive. In the space between those things that impinge on us (stimuli) and our reaction to these things (response), we have the freedom to choose. In other words, we don't have to function on 'autopilot' even though we often do, out of habit. Proactivity is about recognizing our responsibilities and making things happen by using our resourcefulness and initiative. Organizations of every kind can be proactive by combining the creativity and resourcefulness of individuals to create a proactive and entrepreneurial culture within the organization.

2. Begin with the end in mind. Three major components contribute to achievement. The first is leadership, i.e. defining what we want to accomplish. The second is management, i.e. establishing how we can best accomplish it. The third is productivity, i.e. doing it. Beginning with the end in mind gives us direction to guide our activities and is the foundation for leadership. The starting point is to develop a mission statement that will help you focus your activities and priorities. If you find your actions aren't congruent with your mission statement, you can take time out to reflect and improve. All staff should be aligned with the organization's mission. If they are not, they will be a liability rather than an asset to the organization in pursuit of its mission. Thereafter, reward systems must complement and strengthen the stated and implied values systems that underpin the mission.

3. Put first things first. Time management is an essential skill for personal and organizational management. The essence of time management is to organize and act around priorities. There are many books and courses available to help us with our time management. In fact, there are so many that we might be tempted to comment that they must be a waste of time! The essential ingredient of time management is discipline. We all know what we could do to become more effective, so we simply have to do it. But that often requires breaking a few lifelong habits. In essence, the means by which we can effectively put first things first is to (a) prioritize, (b) organize around the priorities, and (c) be disciplined to act in accordance with (a) and (b).

The next three habits explored by Covey deal with social development.

4. Think win–win. Developing win–win performance agreements is the central activity of management and allows staff to manage themselves within the framework of the agreement. This done, the manager's task becomes one of removing or lowering obstacles so that team members can do their jobs unencumbered. Thereafter, the reward systems of the organization will have a strong bearing on the behaviours that are displayed, i.e. what gets rewarded gets done!

5. Seek first to understand then to be understood. When communicating with others, we should first take the time to deeply understand the issues presented to us. If people trust you and believe you understand them, they are more likely to be influenced by what you say. The key skills here are those of good questioning and empathic listening. Empathic listening is listening with intent to understand the other person's frame of reference and feelings. It's about listening with your ears, your eyes and your instincts. Thereafter, knowing how to be understood is as important as seeking to understand when reaching win–win solutions. Using uncluttered language and keeping to the point are essential components. By seeking first to understand and then be understood, you can turn a transactional exchange into a transformational opportunity.

6. Synergize. Covey argues that the application of the first five habits prepares us for synergy. Synergy means the whole is greater than the sum of its parts. Furthermore, the relationship which the parts have to each other is a part in itself. The essence of synergy is to value the mental, emotional and psychological differences between people, build on strengths and compensate for weaknesses. Furthermore, the key to valuing these differences is to realize that all people see the world not as it is, but as they are. We all live inside our own virtual realities.

Covey's seventh habit deals with renewal and creating an upward spiral of growth.

7. Balanced self-renewal. Imagine you've come across someone in the woods who is cutting down a tree with a blunt saw. They are exhausted from working for hours. You suggest they take time out

to sharpen the saw. They might reply, 'I don't have time to sharpen the saw, I'm too busy cutting down trees!' Habit 7 is about taking time to sharpen the saw.

Examples of Covey's described habits are rife in our opening story. The manager is evidencing *'proactivity'* and *'beginning with the end in mind'* (Covey's Habits 1 and 2) through her approach to operational and strategic innovation. However, in relation to her team of stonemasons, her single-minded pursuit of innovation and lack of attention to the concerns expressed by her team members indicate there is little or no application of *'think win–win'* or *'seek first to understand then to be understood'* (Covey's Habits 4 and 5). With the Board of Trustees, she did rather better when presenting her revised vision. Her presentation to them showed clear evidence of *'think win–win'* through the considerations she gave to the range of stakeholder needs and the means by which they would be met under the new scenario. And she listened patiently to the trustees' concerns.

Wayne, from his position of having psychologically withdrawn from the project some time prior to the new manager's arrival, habitually responded to change by taking sick leave. Payne and Jayne showed evidence of exercising the habit of *'beginning with the end in mind'*, i.e. by defining what they each personally wanted to accomplish (accuracy vs quantity respectively). However, the ends each of them had in mind were not aligned with the qualitative and quantitative needs of the organization. And all three stonemasons failed to engage with Habit 5, *'seek first to understand then to be understood'*. Sayne did, however, seek to understand. The problem here lay with the manager, who didn't respond to his requests for information and discussion. I draw special attention to the habit of *'seeking first to understand'* as I believe it signals a good starting point from which we can all improve our working relationships and, thereafter, further explore Covey's remaining six habits.

What follows is an individual reflective exercise. However, if the levels of trust in your team are up to the task, individual reflections can be shared. The aim then would be to deepen your understanding of each other and develop commitment to work better together through the application of new team 'norms' (i.e. team habits!).

Habit 1: Be proactive

- Think of a recent incident when you acted on autopilot. Describe it in detail.

- What was good and what was less so in your behaviours?

- With the benefit of hindsight, what might you have done differently and what result might that have produced?

Habit 2: Begin with the end in mind

- Write down your team's current mission statement. If you don't have one, develop a draft now, for the benefit of this exercise.

- Note three regular (habitual) behaviours that directly support this mission and three that do not directly support it.

- In the light of these thoughts, what might you do differently?

Habit 3: Put first things first

- How do you manage your time and priorities?

- What are the strengths and weaknesses of your approach?

- What can you do to improve your time and priorities management?

Habit 4: Think 'win–win'

- How clear are you about what is expected of you and how closely are rewards linked to achievement of expectations?

- To what degree do these expectations represent a win–win situation for both you and the organization?

- What improvements could you make that would further clarify expectations and more closely link rewards to expected performance?

Habit 5: Seek first to understand and then to be understood

- Describe a situation where you are not currently seeing eye to eye with a work colleague.

- Putting yourself in the other person's shoes, describe the issues from their perspective.

- What approach might you now take towards improving the current situation, i.e. what might you do differently?

Habit 6: Synergize

- What are your particular strengths and weaknesses in relation to your job and working effectively with your colleagues?

- Select three work colleagues. Reflect on how you engage with their particular strengths and weaknesses.

- What might you do differently, and how?

Habit 7: Balanced self-renewal

- Describe the last significant development activity you engaged with.

- In what ways did this activity benefit you and your organization?

- What is your next priority for development? When and how will you take action?

To expand on some of the ideas discussed here, see Aspiration, Goal, Lead, Question, Relationship and Transition.

I

 The key to effective **involve**ment is to engage with those who have the real knowledge and experience.

Involve

Involve *vb*. To include others.

 Deciding on how and when to involve others, or even if I should involve them at all, can be a tricky business. For example, should I involve the family in the decision to take on a new coaching or consultancy contract, paint my office, buy a new car, move house, or go on holiday? The answer as to whether to involve them, and to what degree, lies in an accurate assessment of:

(a) The impact that the decision is likely to have on them, and

(b) The degree to which they have the necessary information/ knowledge to make a meaningful contribution to the decision.

Let's briefly explore the decision to take on a new coaching or consultancy contract. If the contract is local and fits within my normal work pattern, the decision will have little impact on my family and I feel free to make the decision alone. If the contract involves travel to far-off places and associated prolonged periods away from home I feel it appropriate to involve family members in the decision as this will have a significant impact on them. However, to ensure this involvement is meaningful and constructive, I will need to provide them with a few pertinent facts such as the current state of our finances, the frequency of my travels and length of time I'll be away, the potential this new contract has to lead on to other similar contracts, and the alternatives to taking this contract – ideally with a brief cost–benefit analysis associated with each alternative. The better informed they are, and the more the decision impacts upon them, the deeper the involvement should be (even though it does, sometimes, feel easier to make the decision myself).

To what degree can we expect to be involved in decisions about change in our work environment? Where do the real underpinning knowledge and experience lie for making decisions? Where will the real added value come from in the decision-making process? The answers to these questions will depend, of course, on what decisions are being made. Strategic decisions (what we do) are usually the realm of higher-level managers. Operational decisions (how we do it) are usually the realm of managers and staff closer to the action.

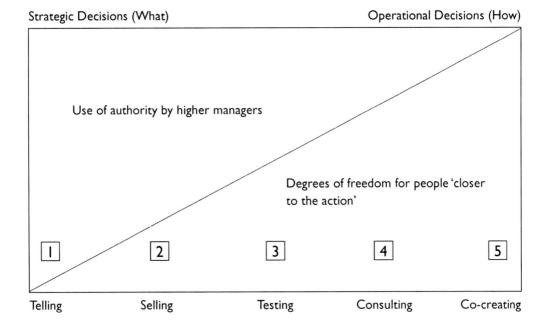

Figure 8: The involvement continuum

Tannenbaum and Schmidt (1973) suggested five levels of involvement, as illustrated in Figure 8.

- **'Hard' Telling:** 'Do it!' The manager makes the full decision and the team simply get on with it – no questions asked.

  'Soft' Telling: 'Okay, here's the problem. Here's the solution. Here's what I want you to do. Now do it!' Again, the manager makes the full decision but in this case provides some context by way of a problem statement. Thereafter, the team simply get on with it – no questions asked.

- **Selling:** 'Here's the problem. These are the options we've considered. These are the reasons we've settled on this solution. Now do it!' The manager explains the context and how the decision has been made – without inviting input.

- **Testing:** 'Here's the problem. These are the alternatives we've considered. We think the right solution is this, for these reasons. But what do *you* think?' If team members offer some compelling arguments to the contrary, the manager may alter the decision.

- **Consulting:** 'Here's the problem. I have some ideas but I'd like to hear from you first.' As team members contribute, the manager fully explores the ideas then concludes by making the final decision him/herself.

- **Co-creating:** 'Here's the problem. Let's make the decision together.' The manager then chairs the discussion. This consensual process requires more time, more interpersonal skill, and more maturity on the part of the group. And it's useful to give people a time window (sunset clause). 'I've only got two weeks. If, by then, we haven't reached agreement, I'll make the decision.' In the end, everyone – including the manager – can say 'I've been heard, I've been understood, and I'm willing to back the decision with a smile.'

The key to effective involvement is to engage with those who have the real knowledge and experience in relation to the decision being made. Therefore, poor decisions are likely to result under two conditions:

- Not involving those who have the appropriate knowledge and/or experience to contribute and, conversely

- Involving those who do not have the appropriate knowledge and/or experience to contribute.

The manager made three key decisions in our scenario:

1. To use new plastic mallets (an operational decision)

2. To abandon building a cathedral and to build an arts and performance centre (a strategic decision)

3. To delay addressing individual variances in performance (an operational decision made by default).

When deciding to adopt the new mallets, the manager involved staff through 'selling': 'Here's the problem' (we have to reduce both our costs and our carbon footprint). 'Here's the solution' (we will adopt new mallets made from recycled plastic). 'Here's how I came to the solution' (these new mallets are half the price and have twice the durability of traditional wooden mallets). Now do it!' The manager explained why the decision had been made – without inviting input. Wayne responded habitually, Payne rejected the approach, Sayne and Jayne accepted it, for reasons explored in more depth elsewhere (see Motivation). The manager might have adopted a 'testing' approach, but this in itself would most likely have generated a similar result. Wayne would probably have avoided engagement with the testing approach, in his habitual manner. Payne, once invited, would have contributed his same objections and the manager would not have found these compelling. Sayne would have engaged enthusiastically in the 'testing' process. Jayne would still have received the idea enthusiastically, i.e. she needed little convincing from her viewpoint. 'Consulting' would have taken much longer, involving, as would be required, much information sharing. It would also have involved an open discussion (maybe confrontation!) of values. As with all decisions, the methodology used will have its own particular set of associated trade-offs.

In proposing the idea to refocus the purpose of the building away from a cathedral and towards an arts and performance centre, the manager adopted a covert 'testing' approach with the Board of Trustees.

Having set the scene at the Exceptional General Meeting, she did not immediately propose her solution. Rather, she gave the trustees time to flounder! She then chose her moment carefully before interjecting with her own solution, as inspired by the story of the Trinity Arts Centre in Tunbridge Wells. And, as with the introduction of the mallets, she did not involve her team of stonemasons in this decision, i.e. she adopted a 'telling' approach. By engaging with Sayne's desire to understand the situation, the manager may have gained some new perspectives. This was yet another lost opportunity with Sayne.

Regarding the decision to delay addressing the individual performance issues of her team of stonemasons (as illustrated in Figure 2), the manager might have usefully adopted a 'co-creating' approach, i.e. worked with each individual to develop a solution while being clear that to do nothing was not an option.

This exercise has two parts, one reflective and one projective. You might carry out the exercise alone, but greater benefits are likely to ensue if you are able to engage your team, in which case the whole exercise should take no more than an hour or so.

First, identify a range of past decisions and slot them into the left-hand column of the template suggested in Figure 9. Thereafter, complete the other columns as appropriate.

Decision made	Background to the decision	Knowledge required to contribute to the decision	Level of involvement that took place	Reflective comments

Figure 9: Analysing a past engagement with the involvement continuum

Now project into the future and consider a range of decisions that are on the horizon. Complete the template in Figure 10.

Decision to be made	Background to the decision	Knowledge required to contribute to the decision	Level of involvement to take place	Comments

Figure 10: Planning a future engagement with the involvement continuum

When completed you might reflect on what you have learned from this exercise.

To expand on some of the ideas discussed here, see Kaizen, Motivation, Power, Relationship and Transition.

J

 In order to avoid becoming **jam**med the combined driving forces of dissatisfaction, a new model of how things will be and a planned process for getting there must be more compelling than the costs associated with the change.

Jam

Jam *vb*. To make or to become stuck.

 I rarely get 'jammed'. Whether innately or through my early childhood experiences, I have always been up for change and always seen the greener grass in the other field. Certainly, in the early stages of my career the prospect of being in the same or a broadly similar job for the next forty years filled me with something close to horror! During these middle stages of my career I have become reasonably content with a relatively stable working situation. This is because this suits me while I experience the rapid and seemingly chaotic changes in family life around me as my children approach their teens. That said, I detect the early signs of itchy feet and am already contemplating what might be next; what options I might have as an 'empty nester' some ten years hence. As I disclosed under Aspiration, I enjoy an ability to visualize my aspirations in detail and 'colour'. I like to build pictures of possible futures. And having a small component of OCD in my nature (maybe those that know me well might prefer the descriptive term 'anorak'!), I am able to organize myself well, i.e. plan, keep things in order and see things through. This happy coming together of attributes (discontentment with the 'here and now', being able to visualize alternative futures and having mild OCD) takes me back to my opening statement – I rarely get jammed.

Organizations and teams become jammed because people, on the whole and within their work environment, are creatures that seek stability and comfort. And we keep doing things the way we always have because we are largely creatures of habit. Furthermore, change involves the belief that there is a better way, and many of us would be uncomfortable with the idea that we may have been doing something suboptimally (wrongly!) for the past few years. What we need in these circumstances is a way of reviewing our current situation that helps create a compelling case for change – a case we can buy into.

As will be explored elsewhere (see Vision), the development of a clear and compelling vision statement is the first step in bringing about change. However, creating a vision is no more than the first step. Michael Beer (1980) offered a perspective on what is required to bring about successful and sustainable change. He used the following formula to summarize a successful change process:

$$\text{Successful change} = (D \times M \times P) > C$$

where:

D = Dissatisfaction with the status quo

M = A new model for how the future could be

P = A planned process for managing change

C = The cost of change to individuals and groups.

Let's explore each of these components in turn.

Dissatisfaction

Dissatisfaction often has its roots in changes in our external operating environment, i.e. changes that we are powerless to control. But if we are unhappy only about things we cannot control, we will quickly feel paralysed to change anything at all – even those things that are within our power to change. So, as a starting point, we have to know what we are dissatisfied with from within the boundaries of our own team or organization. And what's more, we shouldn't be the only person that feels dissatisfied. There has to be enough dissatisfaction within the team as a whole to overcome inertia and energize an effective engagement with change.

A new model

The ideal starting point when creating a new model is a collective vision of how things could be. From this we develop a well-formed mission, i.e. a statement of what we will do to contribute towards the vision becoming a reality. Here are some examples of vision statements and their associated organizational missions:

Vision: A world in which everyone can afford to live in a home they want to live in.

Organizational mission: To provide high quality and affordable homes in the Barnstable area.

Vision: People in the developing world being able to access the learning and development opportunities available from the internet.

Organizational mission: To develop and distribute a portable, solar-powered, $100 computer through the most practical and effective sponsorship means.

Vision: Barcelona at the heart of the European cultural stage.

Organizational mission: To build a world-class arts and performance centre in the heart of the city.

A planned process

Change happens no matter what we do, but bringing about the right change at the right time and at the right pace is the hard part and can only be achieved with careful planning. When a team or organization decides to change, much extra effort is required because customers must still be served, performance and financial targets must still be met, and all stakeholders must still be kept happy. At the same time, team members need to engage with the transitions required to create better ways of doing things (see Transition). If you fail to manage resource, time and transition tensions, the change process will fall apart under the pressure of normal operational demands. The key question that needs to be answered by you and your team is *'How do we stretch even more to bring about this change when we're already stretched so far?'* At least part of the answer to this question will revolve around effective prioritization.

The cost of change

Here we are not talking about a financial cost. We are talking about people's energy and desire to meet the expectations placed on the team during the change process. People become comfortable with long-established ground rules and ways of working. So, when a leader requires a change in these ground rules and, maybe, long-established ways of working, team members are likely to become very uncomfortable. And uncomfortable people resist (see Force). As Michael Beer's equation specifies, in order to avoid becoming jammed the combined driving forces of dissatisfaction, a new model of how things will be and a planned process for getting there must be more compelling than the costs associated with the change. If one of the driving elements is missing, there will be zero value and the resistance to change will be too great. The result of this will be no successful change.

Let's explore one of the two central change situations of our scenario – the adoption of the new mallets. Figure 11 provides a logical structure for our analysis.

Wayne had withdrawn from his work situation because of one or more experiences that preceded the manager's arrival at the Sagrada Familia. Indeed, his withdrawal was so great that he was unable to engage in any change initiative and his energies were directed exclusively towards doing just enough to get by. As stated elsewhere, Wayne remains our unresolved (but not unresolvable) case. Payne was not only satisfied with the continuing use of wooden mallets but, moreover, he identified with the methods of his ancestors and had no intention of breaking with the use of traditional tools and materials. So, no successful change was likely there. Sayne was not overly attached to current working practices and materials and appeared, by nature, to be happy with engaging in informed experimentation. To this end, the manager might have engaged with Sayne in a more inclusive manner. Jayne was dissatisfied with the status quo, i.e. she wanted to see the building project completed within her own lifetime. The introduction of the new mallets was in Jayne's mind accompanied by the possibility of redistributing funds and employing a further stonemason to speed the project along. She became an early adopter of the new mallets. The Board of Trustees was supportive of anything that would progress the project. And the adoption of the new mallets had the added incentive of contributing towards a more environmentally sound operation. From their perspective, the cost of introducing change was nil and there were clear associated benefits.

Forces ☑ Supportive ☒ Resistive ❓ Ambivalent	Change Initiative = The adoption of the new mallets				
	Wayne	**Payne**	**Jayne**	**Sayne**	**The Board**
Dissatisfaction with the status quo	What satisfies and disatisfies Wayne is unclear given his current state of withdrawal. ❓	Payne was very happy with the status quo, i.e. with his mallet that had been used by his father and grandfather. ☒	Jayne had a strong desire to complete the building project, so anything that might speed progress would be welcomed. ✓	Sayne was happy with the status quo, but also curious about the new possibilities. ✓	The Board of Trustees existed to see this whole project through. They would be supportive of anything that might assist. ✓
A new model for how the organization will run	The manager had a clear model as to how this change would improve costs and social responsibility, but Wayne was withdrawn. ❓	The manager's model was not compelling enough for Payne to overcome his attachment to his mallet. ☒	The saving in costs appealed to Jayne enough to gain her enthusiastic support. ✓	Sayne was openminded to the possibilities of the cost/ benefit analysis – but was left uninvolved by the manager. ❓	The manager's model would have appealed to a wide membership of the Board – but they had no need to be involved in this level of detail. ✓
A planned process for managing change	The manager had no planned process other than simply distributing the mallets – but this was not the limiting factor for Wayne. ❓	The manager's crude attempt at selling the concept failed to engage Payne. ☒	Jayne required no more than being given a new mallet along with a simple explanation of cost/benefit. ✓	Sayne was happy to go along with the initiative on a 'try it and see' basis. ✓	Again, the Board had no need to be involved in the detail – a high level cost/ benefit analysis would have been the most they required. ✓
The cost of change to individuals and groups	Wayne was so deeply withdrawn from the project that anything that required him to change would have been too costly. ☒	Payne's potential loss of 'identify' as a master stonemason of three generations' standing was too high a price for him to pay. ☒	The benefit of potentially completing the project sooner greatly outweighed the costs of any change for Jayne. ✓	Sayne was happy to experiment. ✓	From the Board's perspective, only benefits would have been seen. ✓

Figure 11: Engagement with the introduction of new mallets

This exercise has a reflective and a projective component. The time required is likely to be around two hours.

Part 1

First, identify a couple of past change initiatives and describe them briefly in the left-hand column of a template such as that illustrated in Figure 12. Thereafter, complete the other columns as appropriate.

Brief description of change initiative	Levels of dissatisfaction with the pre-change status quo	Quality of planning associated with the implementation of the change	The cost of the change to those involved or affected by the charge

Figure 12: Template for analysing past readiness for change

When you and/or your team have completed this template, you might reflect on what you have learned from this exercise, capturing key points for future reference, i.e. when you engage with Part 2 as described below.

Part 2

Now project into the future and consider a range of change initiatives that are on the horizon. Use the template in Figure 13 as a guide.

Description of proposed change and summary of expected benefits	Current levels of dissatisfaction with the status quo	Quality of current plans to implement the change	The perceived cost of the change to those involved in or affected by the change

Figure 13: Template for analysing future readiness for change

Your reflections on the outputs from this exercise may inform additional actions you will wish to take in order to establish:

- A well-communicated and compelling case for change

- A well-developed action plan

- An involvement exercise that engages all affected people at the appropriate level.

When you have completed this work you might reflect on what you have learned that can be incorporated in an organization-wide set of guidelines for change planning and implementation.

If you don't feel comfortable working with your team right away, you can carry out this exercise alone. But, as with most exercises in this book, greater benefits will follow if you are able to engage your whole team in the learning experience.

 To expand on some of the ideas discussed here, see Aspiration, Force, Habit, Involve, Kaizen, Transition and Vision.

K

Kaizen has emerged as an effective, low-cost, simple, team-based approach to continuous improvement.

Kaizen

Kaizen *vb.* To change (kai) in order to become good (zen) – from Japanese.

I have found reflecting on Kaizen from a personal standpoint to be quite challenging. Indeed, as I pondered this for the first time, I struggled. What tools and techniques do I use, if any, 'to change in order to become good'? How do I measure the degree to which I am continuously improving? In what areas or aspects of my life do I continue to improve? In my infant years I was (as we all were) a master of continuous improvement. During my first three years of life I continuously and rapidly improved in my abilities to communicate, get around, reason, solve problems and work constructively within my environment to get what I needed and wanted. As time passed, the ways in which I continuously improved became less spectacular. In my early career, developing my scientific/ technical knowledge and experience was paramount. Then learning how to effectively lead a team took centre stage. Nowadays, developing as an ever more effective coach and group facilitator is my key focus. My challenge is to recognize and engage in ever more subtle continuous improvement!

 After World War II the Japanese adopted 'quality' as their key philosophy for economic recovery. In line with a traditional Japanese approach, they sought seven tools to accomplish their economic rejuvenation (a Japanese samurai carried seven tools into battle). The seven tools chosen were:

- Histograms

- Graphs

- Cause and effect diagrams

- Control charts

- Check sheets

- Scatter diagrams

- Pareto diagrams.

These tools were developed as aids to the process of statistical quality control and within Kaizen organizations all personnel are trained to use these tools, with the resulting charts and diagrams being displayed prominently.

Since those early days of the 1940s and 50s, Kaizen has emerged as an effective, low-cost, simple, team-based approach to continuous improvement. Typically, teams are trained in the techniques and tools of Kaizen and form themselves into quality circles. The members of the quality circles brainstorm improvement ideas and vote on them for priority action. They then create an action plan which is submitted to management for approval. Once approved, the team sets about implementation (with professional help if appropriate). The team continues to meet at appropriate intervals to review progress, identify and overcome barriers, celebrate successes, and document the resulting changed processes. Hence, the 'Kaizen attitude' supports a continuous process of incremental improvement with all members of a team expected to be involved. Managers are expected to spend about half their time on improving upon what they and their teams do. This creates a proactive culture which recognizes that improvements can be small or large and that many small improvements can make a big difference.

At its most basic level of analysis, Kaizen is grounded in two principles:

- Change for the better

- Continuity.

A system or culture that lacks either of these is not true Kaizen. Maintaining existing ways of working (good though they may be) lacks the essential 'change for the better' element, though it does ensure continuity. Similarly, an overly vigorous approach to change, not backed up by the maintenance of what currently works well, lacks the element of continuity. At a detailed level Kaizen works through the following principles:

1.   Be prepared to discard conventional fixed ideas.

2.   Think of *how it can be done*, not *why it can't be done*.

3.   Start by questioning current practices.

4.   Don't make excuses.

5.   Don't seek perfection. Do it right away even if it will only achieve 50 per cent of the target.

6.   If you make a mistake, correct it right away.

7.   Throw wisdom at a problem, not money.

8.   Ask 'Why?' five times in order to seek root causes.

9.   Seek the wisdom of ten people rather than the knowledge of one.

10.   Go back to point 1 and start again!

The construction manager showed little evidence of Kaizen-style working. She did collect performance data and organized it within a table but her activity stopped there. In the spirit of Kaizen, the next step would have been to present the data to her team members and begin to solicit their interest in understanding root causes and working towards improvements. On the back of an initial team meeting, she would have introduced regular work-related improvement meetings, supported by appropriate training in problem-solving and decision-making techniques. In this way, the seeds of a culture of continuous improvement would have been sown and a *team* would have been created! And with the formation of a team, the manager would have introduced a significant additional resource for improved performance management, i.e. peer pressure.

Peer pressure within our group of stonemasons may have assisted in the management of sickness absence, improving the quality of work and/or improving productivity. Most often when we hear of peer pressure it is associated with negative connotations, e.g. the pressure exerted on teenagers to take drugs or the pressure in the workplace to 'work to rule'. But peer pressure can work for the good of an individual or group. Clearly, this is what the manager of the Gaudi project would wish to support. Good peer pressure is facilitated when a team leader:

- Maintains a style of behaviour that leads by positive example

- Confronts performance issues as they occur

- Promotes teamworking by providing the appropriate time and resources for initiatives such as Kaizen.

Two or three hours will be needed for this activity.

1. Following an introduction to Kaizen (the notes at the beginning of this section may assist here), place six sheets of flipchart paper around the walls, each with one of the questions below as its header:

    - How do we currently go about having discussions that lead to work-related improvements?

    - To what degree does our team use up-to-date data and facts for making decisions?

- What tools and techniques do we use for the purpose of continuous improvement?

- To what degree is our team empowered to implement any ideas we generate?

- How good are our team's cross-functional links with other teams?

- What improvements has our team introduced over the past year and what benefits have we seen from these?

2. Ask team members to write their responses to each question on post-it notes and stick them to the appropriate sheet on the wall. Responses should describe the current situation rather than simply being one- or two-word answers. And encourage team members to provide specific examples where possible.

3. When everyone has contributed to each sheet, allocate a sheet to each individual (if six or fewer team members are taking part) or to small groups (if seven or more are taking part). Ask them to review and organize the post-its and develop a comprehensive and ordered summary on their allocated flipchart sheet.

4. These summaries should then be fed back to the full group and discussed. Following each discussion, note any goals the team agree to work towards in relation to that particular sheet, with a particular emphasis on improving the current situation. Once all sheets have been covered, stand back and draw out priorities for action. If time permits, carry out a team coaching exercise on one or more of the priority goals (see Coach). If time is short, return as a group in the near future and carry out the coaching exercise. Alternatively, small groups may take one or two goals each, and return a week or so later with the results.

To expand on some of the ideas discussed here, see Balance, Coach, Delegate, Involve and Zen.

L

 Leadership and management are things we do, rather than positions we occupy.

Lead

Lead *vb.* To show the way to an individual or a group by going ahead.

 Here I began my reflections with the question 'Am I a natural leader?' This raised the question 'What does it mean to be a leader?' When I gained my first leadership position, the most helpful criticism I received was during my annual appraisal with my then boss, Bob. He said that over the past year, the most disappointing aspect of my behaviour was that when he spoke with me, he felt as if he was speaking with one of my team members. I was accused of 'staying native' with my team, rather than promoting the leadership and performance agenda of the organization. The most rewarding feedback I received was just a year later, when Bob praised me for leading by example, i.e. modelling the behaviours I wished to see in my team. These were two highly significant pieces of feedback for me.

Reflecting on these early experiences of myself 'doing' leadership was interesting, but still didn't answer the question of whether I am a natural leader (or not!). Observing my children growing up, my older daughter showed clear leadership traits by the age of three. She naturally and enthusiastically took the lead in activities with her friends and most of those around her would be content to follow. My younger daughter began to show her leadership traits at around the age of six. Her style was to lead in a quiet but assertive manner that was characterized as much by what she would not do as by what she would do. She influenced others in her peer group in a calm way, rather than by standing out.

In terms of my natural style, I am enthusiastic about anything new and like immersing myself in a challenge. I also enjoy problem solving and develop vivid pictures of how things could be and how that might be achieved. These attributes can serve me well as a leader, but they can also make me bossy, autocratic, impatient and overly ambitious. Experience has taught me that the degree to which I express 'good' leadership skills and behaviours is greatly influenced by the situations I find myself in. I have benefited enormously from a few significant developmental experiences, two of which were described in the opening paragraph to this section. Of further significance for me was the mentoring relationship that my line manager offered me during my two years in Shell Ventures; and another was skippering my yacht during particularly bad weather in the North Sea. The benefit of reflecting on such experiential learning is that it has enabled me to develop context-related leadership behaviours.

According to McGregor (1987), leadership is not a property of the individual, but a complex relationship among the following variables:

- The characteristics of the leader

- The attitudes, needs and other personal characteristics of the followers

- The nature of the organization, such as its purpose, its structure, and the tasks to be performed

- The social, economic and political environment in which leadership is being practised.

Hollingsworth defined leadership as much from the perspective of what it isn't as from the perspective of what it is. For example:

The Differences between Management and Leadership

- A manager administers – a leader innovates

- A manager maintains – a leader develops

- A manager focuses on systems and structure – a leader focuses on people

- A manager relies on control – a leader inspires trust

- A manager keeps an eye on the bottom line – a leader has an eye on the horizon

- A manager does things right – a leader does the right thing.

(Hollingsworth, 1999, pp. 22–3)

Miller et al. focused on a distinction between 'things' and 'people':

Management involves using human, equipment, information and other resources to achieve various objectives. On the other hand, leadership focuses on getting things done through others. Thus, you manage things (budgets, procedures and so on), but you lead people.

(Miller et al., 1996, p. 249)

Having considered these different views we might conclude that leadership and management are things we do, rather than positions we occupy.

Accepting this proposition, and building on McGregor's 'complex relationship' description of leadership, it is the integration of our behaviours with the needs of team members, the culture of our organizations and the demands of the external environment that are critical to our success as leaders. Situational leaders/managers adapt their style and behaviours to the circumstances in which they find themselves. In the remainder of this section, we will restrict ourselves to an exploration of ourselves in relation to our team members.

The concept of situational behaviour was popularized in the 1960s and 1970s by the Situational Leadership theories of Hersey and Blanchard. In the model they constructed, successful leadership behaviour is contingent upon the maturity and competence of followers, i.e. their level of independence in relation to the role they occupy. In Figure 14 I have adapted their model in the light of my own experiences as a leader and as a coach to leaders.

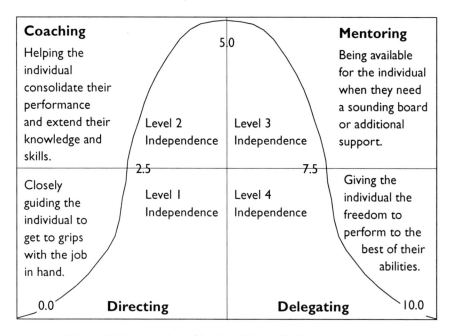

Figure 14: Four styles of leadership available to a manager

The independence that team members display may be divided into four levels as follows:

Level 1 – Low independence: The appropriate leadership style emphasizes task-oriented *directive* behaviours, i.e. providing specific instructions and closely supervising performance.

Level 2 – Low to moderate independence: The appropriate leadership style emphasizes both task- and relationship-oriented behaviours in equal measure, i.e. a *coaching* style that involves asking questions aimed at checking understanding and exploring approaches to be adopted. The main drive is still provided by the leader.

Level 3 – Moderate to high independence: The appropriate leadership style emphasizes two-way communication and supportive behaviours, i.e. a *mentoring* style that involves sharing ideas and being available to support when required. Here the drive in the relationship is no longer primarily from the leader, but from the team member who requests support at their own discretion.

Level 4 – High independence: The appropriate leadership style is characterized by the establishment of a guiding vision to which team members are able to sign up. Beyond this, a *delegatory* style would be appropriate as little direction or support are required. The leader is able to fully turn responsibility over to highly able, experienced and motivated followers.

The matching of leadership style to the needs of followers is critical if we are to avoid both abandoning staff when they need more support and over-managing staff when they are able and willing to occupy positions of greater independence.

Even superficial analysis of day-to-day performance suggests that Wayne, Payne, Sayne and Jayne each required quite different leadership styles if they were to become fully effective employees. Wayne, though probably capable of being led by way of a *delegatory* style (his performance against accuracy and quantity targets was spot on), needed constant and focused attention on his habitual sickness absence. Payne appeared highly independent in his role, working to very fine tolerances during his block production activities. However, the number of blocks he produced was an issue requiring focused attention. In a virtual mirror image of Payne, Jayne's enthusiasm resulted in her exceeding her quantity targets, but she failed to meet quality requirements. Using a *delegatory* style in these instances simply resulted in the maintenance of an unacceptable, and deeply entrenched, status quo. By contrast, Sayne – as a highly able and independent worker – did require a delegatory style of leadership. The challenge associated with leading Sayne would be to maintain his high levels of motivation in a context that no longer stretches him. Should he desire it (and there's every indication that he would), additional responsibilities could be delegated to Sayne to prepare him for promotion. The further challenge, for some managers, would be to support him in gaining employment as a manager elsewhere if there were no timely succession opportunities within the current team or organization.

Regarding performance during the two change initiatives, the manager adopted a universal *directive* style. This resulted in Wayne's absence from work along with Payne's and Jayne's resignations. Almost certainly, this directive style of leadership will eventually have eroded Sayne's enthusiasm for the job as well. The use of a *mentoring* style, with its requirement for the drive to be provided by the person being led, would probably have yielded a similar result. This leaves us with the option of applying a *coaching* style. By engaging in coaching-style discussions, at the right time and place, the team could have explored actual versus required behaviours, identified barriers to the meeting of targets and generated solutions which could then be applied in partnership. A more detailed treatment of this approach is to be found in the Coach and Question sections.

What follows is an individual reflective exercise. However, if the levels of trust in your team are up to the task, individual reflections can be shared. The aim would be to deepen your understanding of each other and develop personal commitments to work better together, thus establishing new team norms.

As suggested under Level 4 independence above, when exploring the appropriate leadership style to be applied to individuals and teams, it is useful to consider three key variables. These are:

- **Ability:** The knowledge, expertise, talent and skills required to do the job

- **Experience:** The track record of the individual in the kind of work in question, combined with skills learned elsewhere that can be transferred

- **Motivation:** The self-generated drive, confidence and energy directed towards taking responsibility for tasks and accountabilities.

Using the template illustrated in Figure 15, make an assessment of these variables for three of your team members.

	Ability	Experience	Motivation
	Score each out of 10		
Person 1			
Person 2			
Person 3			

Figure 15: Analysing the independence levels of team members

Motivation itself can be seen to be a function of three further situational attributes:

- **Clarity:** How clear is the individual about what is expected in terms of their approach, behaviour and achievement?

- **Reality:** How realistic is the expectation being placed on the individual in the light of other demands and their levels of ability and experience?

- **Value:** How much does the individual value achieving the expected outcome(s).

We will expand on this concept in the next section (see Motivation), but for now, as with the exercise above, make an assessment of these variables for the same three team members, using Figure 16 as your guide.

	Clarity	Reality	Value
	Score each out of 10		
Person 1			
Person 2			
Person 3			

Figure 16: Analysing the motivation levels of team members

Having carried out these preliminary diagnostics, further reflect upon underlying causes that may account for the scores you have allocated. Thereafter, engage in a coaching-style discussion with your team members and establish an action plan for each that takes account of your raised awareness. Ideally, you will have shared the notes in this section and given your team members the opportunity to complete the exercise from their own perspectives prior to your one-to-one meeting. In this case, your discussion will begin with a comparison of scores. Both similarities and differences can be explored and, if conducted in the spirit of sharing and extending your understanding of each other, this will make for a highly productive contribution to reviewing and enhancing your working relationships. This can all take place within an established schedule of one-to-one/supervisory meetings if appropriate. Or it may be the trigger for establishing regular one-to-ones.

To expand on some of the ideas discussed here, see Aspiration, Coach, Delegate, Motivation, Question and Relationship.

M

 In principle, there are three ways to create a high level of **motivation** in a team.

Motivation

Motivation *vb.* The self-generated confidence and energy that is directed towards doing something.

 All the things I do, I do because there is either an associated gain or an associated avoidance of pain. Some gains or avoidances of pain are material, some non-material, occasionally both. But they are never immaterial! Furthermore, avoidance of pain is itself a reward, so for me it all comes down to associated rewards. This could be a place to explore altruism, i.e. do I help the older person cross the road – when I'm already late for my train – because I genuinely wish to help them, or because I'll later struggle with the guilt of not having helped them? No doubt a very rapid cost–benefit analysis will take place in my subconscious as I make what appears to be a spontaneous decision to help or walk on by! But no more of this here; I'll simply engage with the proposition that the degree to which I am motivated towards a particular behavioural response or course of action will depend upon the value of the reward to me over and above the costs associated with the effort I need to invest. Furthermore, I am also affected by how clear I am about what I am aiming for and how realistic I perceive my chances of success to be. These issues were touched upon during my earlier reflections on Aspiration.

Motivating staff to provide their best efforts in working towards organizational goals is one of the universal challenges for managers and leaders. This challenge is exacerbated by the common misconception that people join organizations to pursue the organization's goals. The fact is that most people join organizations to pursue their own goals.

In principle, there are three ways to create a high level of motivation in a team:

1.   Employ only those people whose goals are completely aligned with those of the organization

2.   Employ people whose goals are broadly aligned with those of the organization and then shape these employees through training, socialization, or other means

3.   Create the conditions within the organization that enable people to align their needs with those of the organization.

Approach 1 is all but impossible. Approach 2 relies on the effectiveness of training programmes and appealing to a 'herd instinct' that is not common among employees in the 21st century. Approach 3 is, therefore, the only solution left. But what does it mean to 'create the conditions' for high motivation within an organization? As explained elsewhere (see Aspiration and Lead), motivation is a function of three situational attributes:

•   **Clarity:** How clear is the individual about what is expected in terms of their approach, behaviour and achievement?

•   **Reality:** How realistic is the expectation being placed on the individual in the light of other demands and their levels of ability and experience?

•   **Value:** How much does the individual value achieving the expected outcome(s)?

'Clarity' and 'reality' are largely in the domain of the manager's responsibilities. Managers need to feel confident that their individual team members, and their teams as a whole, are clear about what is expected of them, and that what is expected of them is realistic. Beyond this, we move into 'value', which is an area of shared responsibility. The degree to which a team member will value achieving what is expected of them will be related to the relevance to themselves of the outcome of their performance. If I deeply value facilitating an organization's development, and the goals I'm set as a consultant are clear and realistic, I'm likely to be highly motivated in working towards my goals, assuming the values underpinning current organization development practices are aligned with my personal values. If, on the other hand, I don't value selling slightly dodgy cars to people who are using their hard-earned savings to buy what they hope is the car of their dreams, I'm not likely to be a good second-hand car salesman (unless I'm desperate for the money and fear losing my job if I don't perform to target. And to those second-hand car salesmen reading this who don't sell slightly dodgy second-hand cars … please forgive me!). We will explore these concepts in more depth as we consider the Gaudi scenario.

As ever, Wayne is the character we can say least about, given we know so little about him from our opening story. He is evidently clear about the technical requirements of the job – he produces the targeted number of blocks each day at the required size tolerances. What he does seem to be unclear about is acceptable levels of sickness absence. His current level of 24 days is way over the organization's target limit of a maximum of eight days per annum. The appropriate course of action here might be to speak with Wayne to ensure he is aware of the organizational standard he is breaching. If he is, it may be that a lack of management concern in the past has led him to hold no value in maintaining this standard. If, on exploring Wayne's issues, the manager is unable to help Wayne find value in appropriate attendance at work, the coercive approach associated with a disciplinary code might be required. In other words, if Wayne won't turn up to work for the sake of getting the cathedral (or arts centre) built, he may turn up in order to keep his job! This is clearly not a very good state of affairs as it appears to address the symptoms rather than the underlying causes of Wayne's behaviour. As such it is unlikely to result in sustainable change.

Neither Payne nor Jayne valued achieving the 'balanced' result of ten blocks per day sized to within +/– 10mm tolerances. Payne focused on accuracy at the expense of speed while Jayne focused on speed at the expense of accuracy. This gives a clue as to where their respective motivations lie. And given that their motivations were so deeply associated with their personal values (Payne to maintain his identity as a master stonemason and Jayne to get the cathedral completed within her lifetime for the use of her family), the manager faced a major challenge in bringing these two in line.

Sayne's motivation remained high throughout our opening story. But how long would this continue? Was he ready to be developed into a management position?

We have already begun our explorations of motivation (see the exercises associated with Aspiration and Lead). Here we will build on these exercises by diagnosing your organization's motivation and reward systems. As with many exercises in The Knowledge, this can be carried out alone by reflecting on your own knowledge and experience or it may be carried out with your team within the context of a team development session. For the latter, simply present the notes below on a series of flip charts or on a set of PowerPoint slides and allow your team members to brainstorm their responses. Accept all responses at face value in the first instance and then refine them once you have worked through all of the categories. An action plan should emerge at the end of the session. As a team exercise, up to two hours may be required.

Consider and make brief notes on the following:

- What rewards offered by your organization are of value in getting individuals to contribute their best efforts in achieving the team's aims? The following categories may help you in your reflections:

  - Economic incentives such as pay and benefits
  - Symbols of prestige and status
  - Informal job content such as freedom, recognition and interesting work.

- How is each of the rewards you have identified obtained? Is it for:

  - Individual performance (e.g. via individual appraisal)?
  - Team performance (e.g. via team performance review)?

- Fixed membership (e.g. automatically awarded to all staff)?
- Variable membership (e.g. long-service staff only)?
- Level (e.g. given automatically to those at a certain level in the hierarchy)?
- Attendance (e.g. for simply turning up for work!)?

- Having reflected on these points, what actions could you take to:

    - Maximize the benefits of current reward systems in the management of your team?
    - Minimize the weaknesses of current reward systems in the management of your team?
    - Have a positive influence on the reward systems currently adopted by your organization?

 To expand on some of the ideas discussed here, see Aspiration, Coach, Goal, Involve, Lead and Relationship.

N

Narratives have a systemic nature. They offer us a means of turning isolated concepts, facts and experiences into an understanding of how the world works in a complex and multifaceted manner.

Narrative

Narrative *n*. An account or story of events, experiences, etc.

When I meet up with friends, particularly those I only see once or twice a year, we always spend some time reminiscing. We talk of times, events, people and paths taken 'when we were younger'. Why? Well, I have my answer to that question! Going back over some of the old stories helps us place our current situations and circumstances in a broader context. It helps us chart where we've come from, where we are now, and where we might be headed. Sometimes I feel really good after a particularly vivid session of story-telling. I also enjoy listening to my friends' narratives, particularly when they have a strong message for me personally. And given they are my friends, I am in a good empathic space from the start.

Mark Friedman (2005) promotes the telling of 'the story behind the baseline' of performance data. I recommend him to you wholeheartedly.

In the introduction to this book I made the point that stories (or narratives) offer us a means to see and understand our individual worlds in new and enlightened ways. Long before the invention of the printing press and the beginning of formal education, narratives were the means by which information and wisdom were passed from one generation to the next. Whether they described real events, parables or incorporated both (as in our current apocryphal tale of the building of the Sagrada Familia), stories were the main tool for teaching and learning. In the 21st century, narratives remain a key component of teaching, be this as a part of primary education where they are used to introduce morals and teach the rules of society, or secondary and tertiary education where, in the form of case studies, they provide a rich context for applying newly learned concepts and skills. As adults, we may still be influenced, on a mass scale, by stories. Millions of people around the world watch serial dramas or 'soap operas'. Typically, these are populated with characters that have an affinity with the viewers, facing challenges and situations familiar to theirs. Such characters often fall into three broad categories: positive role models whose behaviour results in good things; negative role models whose behaviour has adverse effects on themselves and others; and transitional role models who start out negatively but turn into positive role models by the end, or vice versa. By watching these dramas, society at large is able to explore topics of the day and learn from the (fictitious) experiences of others.

Finally, narratives have a systemic nature. They offer us a means of turning isolated concepts, facts and experiences into an understanding of how the world works in a complex and multifaceted manner. Real learning is not about knowing something, it's about understanding it within its worldly context.

I mentioned above the categories of role model that often appear in TV dramas – the negative, positive and transitional role models. In our opening story, all characters have the potential to fall into any one of these categories. Through these A to Z sections we are exploring the various factors that could push them into each category. For example, Wayne makes his first appearance as a negative role model. But if we take the time to understand the background to his current situation he may become a transitional character as we find ways to encourage him into the positive role model category. The jury is still out on this one.

Payne appears to be in the positive role model category when we first encounter him. But by our second encounter, when he responds negatively to operational change, we have to reframe our experience of him. Likewise with Jayne, who comes across as a positive role model in both the opening encounter and the one concerning the adoption of the new mallets. However, her response to the change of final purpose for the Sagrada Familia may leave us feeling ambivalent. On the one hand we might think of her as being highly principled and authentic, or on the other as narrowly focused and short-sighted.

Sayne maintains his status as a positive role model throughout. But we wonder how long this will remain so, given the manager's behaviours towards him.

The construction manager enters the story as a positive role model. However, she transitions into a negative role model through a series of behaviours that lose her the team – if indeed there ever was a team.

In this exercise we will further explore the value of stories through the medium of a TV drama.

1. Bring the team together within an environment conducive to being creative. Ask team members to recall a range of TV drama series and comment on their favourites. Examples may include series such as Cold Feet, The Wire, Shameless, Life on Mars, Desperate Romantics, etc. You might also consider which of the main TV channels broadcast these dramas, i.e. whether each channel has its own distinctive style.

2. Provide subgroups of two to five team members, depending on the overall size of the team, with a sheet of flipchart paper and a range of coloured pens.

3. Ask each group to create a template for a six-square storyboard or 'comic strip' by first sketching six squares on the flipchart paper.

4. Then ask each group to populate the template with the story of the team from some given point in the past to the present day.

Essentially, this involves creating a simple line drawing (artistic merit is not important) and short narrative in each square. The storyboard can be given a title and, if you wish to really enter the spirit of the exercise, the TV channel which would most likely screen the drama!

5. Each group should then present their narrative to the full team. This is likely to be a fun exercise that contains some significant points for the team leader to note.

6. Following the presentations, provide each group with another sheet of flipchart paper and ask them to divide this into six squares as before.

7. Now each group should write the sequel to the first series, ending at some agreed point in the future such that there is a realistic, best outcome for the team.

8. Each group then presents its sequel to the full team. Let discussions run their course.

9. Draw out themes and potential goals for the team.

10. As a full team, agree goals to be taken forward and allocate these to subgroups who can apply a team coaching exercise to the goals and present appropriate action plans back to the full team.

 To expand on some of the ideas discussed here, see Coach, Options, Scenario, Vision and Walkabout.

O

The effect of habitually making instinctive decisions is to undermine our ability to distinguish those instances when a more robust **option** generation approach is necessary.

Option

Option *n*. That which is available from a range of alternatives.

Having options, for me, is synonymous with having a sense of freedom. Certainly, if I have no options I feel trapped or imprisoned. But with options I sense I have a degree of self-determination; I don't feel 'determined'. I'll relate this to my career path. I have never been made redundant, but I have experienced reaching the end of a number of time-limited assignments. The first of these was when I reached the end of my two-year secondment as part of Shell International's Group Planning team. The expected place for me to go on completion of this secondment was back to my role as an environmental microbiologist in Shell Research. But that didn't feel good to me – note my use of the phrase '*back* to my role …'! So I actively sought options. This led me to a further secondment, in Shell Ventures, exploring Shell's options to develop new business opportunities. Other options available to me at this time included teaching, voluntary service overseas, travelling, etc. Given that I settled on another secondment within Shell, I was again faced with 'going back' some twenty months later. More options were explored and these resulted in me taking a position within a business development agency in Kent – and so the story continues. The key for me is that I have never felt like a victim of circumstance. I've maintained a sense of freedom.

So, what are my current options? To continue with my coaching, leadership and organization development work; to seek full-time employment with a particular organization; to retrain into a new profession (teaching still appeals); to walk the Earth in the spirit of Cain. Already I am again feeling an immense sense of freedom! But, as I type this, with the children at school and the sun shining in the garden outside, I feel quite content on my current path. So I'll keep going for a little longer – unless circumstances call me to reconsider.

 Generally, as managers, we're not good at working with options. We make numerous decisions every day and the vast majority of these are made on the hoof. We simply don't have the time to generate a range of options, carry out a cost–benefit analysis and then put together an implementation plan for each decision we have to make. What we do is carry out a largely preconscious analysis and go with 'what seems right'. Although this is often the most effective approach to day-to-day decision making (a good-enough decision made in good time is better than a perfect decision made too late!), the effect of habitually making instinctive decisions is to undermine our ability to identify those instances when a more robust option generation approach is necessary.

Many readers will be familiar with the principles and practice of SWOT analysis (strengths, weaknesses, opportunities, threats) as originally developed by Ansoff (1987). In my experience this is a highly underutilized tool. Typically, SWOT analysis will be carried out as part of a business planning exercise where it provides a snapshot of the current situation both within and outside of the business. The method involves drawing up a four-box grid (see examples later) and populating this with the brainstormed thoughts of team members. Thereafter, a further brainstorming session suggests actions that might be taken to maximize strengths, compensate for weaknesses, defend against threats and optimize opportunities. SWOT's key benefit when used in this way is to identify issues for discussion and debate. The typical shortfall is that discussions tend to be hard to focus and often the final outputs can be too vague to be of actionable value.

To add further value to a SWOT analysis, we can extend the technique to include a structured option generation activity. This requires us to compare pairs of SWOT statements. For example, the first *'Opportunities'* statement is compared with the first *'Strengths'* statement and team members are asked to generate one or more ideas to exploit this combination. Thereafter different pairs of statements are combined and the process continues until all possible combinations have been explored. This provides a comprehensive and wide-ranging reservoir of options for the team or organization to explore further through individual or team coaching exercises (see Coach).

Furthermore, this SWOT and option generation technique need not be restricted to business planning exercises. The techniques are applicable to just about any decision that needs to be made.

Here we will explore the application of SWOT and option generation to the behaviour and performance issues confronting the new manager.

One of the key criticisms we might aim at the manager is her failure to address each of the stonemasons' individual performance issues. If the manager had taken some quality time for reflection and carried out a SWOT analysis on her staff, the result may have looked something like the illustration provided in Figure 17, in which I have restricted myself to a consideration of just two of her team members.

Strengths	Weakness	Strengths	Weakness
Wayne maintains an excellent balance between accuracy and productivity in his work	Wayne has an unacceptable sickness absence record	Jayne is highly committed to Gaudi's vision and is a good communicator	Jayne cannot see the bigger picture and works quickly but not accurately
Opportunities	Threats	Opportunities	Threats
Wayne could be a benchmark for continuous improvement projects	A poor attendance culture may develop across the team if Wayne is left unchecked	Jayne could become more accurate and still produce a higher than target number block	Jayne inadvertently slows progress by continuing to produce substandard blocks

Figure 17: A SWOT analysis on two stonemasons' approaches to work

The challenge now is for the manager to take timely and appropriate action in the light of this analysis. What follows in Figures 18 and 19 are illustrations of options that might be generated by a structured approach to comparing paired statements from the SWOT analysis of Wayne and Jayne respectively.

	Strengths Wayne maintains an excellent balance between accuracy and productivity in his work	Weakness Wayne has an unacceptable sickness absence record
Opportunities Wayne could be a benchmark for continuous improvement projects	Encourage Wayne to actively engage with continuous improvement initiatives – maybe 'chair' a group	Engage with Wayne in a coaching relationship that explores the underlying causes of his attitudes
Threats A poor attendance culture may develop across the team if Wayne is left unchecked	The manager to develop a teamworking approach aimed at improving quality and productivity	The manager to make clear her expectations and use disciplinary procedures if necessary

Figure 18: Option generation grid to address Wayne's operational performance

The approach to Wayne could begin with the manager making clear her expectations of performance. Thereafter she could offer Wayne the option to engage in a coaching relationship that explored the underlying causes of his negative attitude to work and poor attendance record. Assuming progress was made, the next option would be to encourage Wayne to capitalize on his consistent on-target performance by engaging in continuous improvement initiatives. If this path failed, the manager would need to engage in formal disciplinary procedures.

The approach to Jayne, as with the previous illustration, should begin with the manager making her expectations of performance clear. Thereafter the manager could explore with Jayne the effects of her focus on quantity at the expense of quality, i.e. blocks have to be reworked before they can be used in the construction of the cathedral. This option appears twice in the options grid below, suggesting this may be a critical option to follow with Jayne. If Jayne engages with this, the manager might then explore with Jayne the number of blocks she can produce at a range of accuracy levels. And, as with Wayne, if this supportive approach to Jayne fails, the manager would need to engage with formal disciplinary procedures.

	Strengths Jayne is highly committed to Gaudi's vision and is a good communicator	Weakness Jayne cannot see the bigger picture and works quickly but not accurately
Opportunities Jayne could become more accurate and still produce a higher than target number of blocks	Work with Jayne to explore the number of blocks she could produce at different levels of accuracy	Explain to Jayne that her focus on quantity at the expense of accuracy is slowing the project down
Threats Jayne inadvertently slows progress by continuing to produce substandard blocks	Explain to Jayne that her focus on quantity at the expense of accuracy is slowing the project down	The manager to make clear her expectations and use disciplinary procedures if necessary

Figure 19: Option generation grid to address Jayne's operational performance

In both cases above, formal discipline is the final and undesirable option. However, if progress is not forthcoming from the alternative approaches, a failure to engage with formal discipline will almost certainly lead to longer-term frustrations and dysfunctional behaviours within the team – as many who read this may have experienced in their own workplaces.

There are two options available to you in exploring the use of SWOT analysis and option generation. The first is to carry out an individual exercise targeted on the individuals in your team, as illustrated above. The second is to carry out a team exercise related to an issue of interest to all team members.

Option 1: An individual exercise

1.   Draw up a four-box SWOT grid for each of your team members, as illustrated earlier in relation to Wayne and Jayne.

2.   Brainstorm your thoughts about each team member using the SWOT boxes as a prompt. Guidelines for brainstorming are as follows:

     •   'Free-wheel' your thoughts, i.e. go with your natural flow of thoughts
     •   Go for quantity rather than quality
     •   Get your thoughts down quickly
     •   No enlargement necessary
     •   State the obvious
     •   Don't fear repetition.

3.   Once you have run out of steam with your brainstorm, reflect on your output and transfer your considered thoughts on the strengths, weaknesses, opportunities and threats associated with each of your team members into an option-generating grid (use the illustrations provided in Figures 18 and 19 as a guide).

4.   Start generating some options! As these emerge from the exercise, you might develop them into clearly stated goals and carry out a coaching exercise on each (see Coach).

Option 2: A team exercise

This should be focused on an area or issue of particular interest to you and your team, e.g. the organization's competitive position, the team's ability to innovate, the team's responsiveness to change, or simply teamworking. The steps are similar to those outlined for Option 1.

1.   Bring your team together. Three to four hours will be required for the full exercise.

2.   Explain the techniques you'll be using (maybe refer to the opening notes of this section as a guide).

3.   Agree on a focus for your SWOT analysis (e.g. the organization's competitive position, the team's ability to innovate, etc.).

4.   Draw up a four-box SWOT grid on a sheet of flipchart paper and write the chosen focus at the top of the sheet.

5. Provide all team members with a wad of post-it notes and ask them to brainstorm their thoughts and then stick their post-its onto the appropriate square of the SWOT grid (reinforce the guidelines for brainstorming as provided earlier).

6. Once the team has run out of steam with the brainstorm, allocate one box of the SWOT grid to each team member (if four or fewer team members are present) or to subgroups (if five or more team members are present).

7. Ask each team member or subgroup to reflect on their allocated post-its and organize the information so that it can be written into an option generation grid and fed back to the rest of the group (this grid will need to be prepared on a sheet of flipchart paper using the illustrative templates provided in Figures 18 and 19).

8. Allow the team a generous amount of time to discuss and expand upon the material generated. Capture important additional points as they arise.

9. Return to brainstorming mode with the team, again using post-it notes but with the focus this time being on generating options to go into the options grid so that paired components of the SWOT analysis are being compared.

10. Once the team has run out of steam with this second brainstorm exercise, allocate one box from the options grid to each team member or subgroup and ask them to organize the options and feed them back to the rest of the group.

11. Again, allow the team a generous amount of time to discuss the options and capture important additional points as they arise.

12. Agree options and allocate as appropriate to individuals or subgroups for them to use as the subject for a coaching exercise (see Coach). The coaching exercise can take place as part of this event, or be carried out back in the workplace for presentation at a future reconvening of the team – but not too far in the future!

To expand on some of the ideas discussed here, see Coach, External, Motivation, Scenario and Unique.

P

 We each have six sources of **power** available to us. Our wise engagement with these can greatly enhance our influence over others.

Power

Power *n.* The exercise of control, influence or authority.

 The way I influence those around me varies in accordance with the context within which I am operating. In personal relationships, my innate curiosity about others can make me rewarding company for those I meet and, because of this, I am able to exercise a degree of influence. But if I over-indulge my curiosity I can appear nosey or sycophantic. Thereafter I lose my reward-based influence. In my professional relationships my expertise comes to the fore, i.e. I am able to influence people because of my experience and/or what I know. In other words, I use my expert power. At other times, and depending on context, I may use my coercive or legitimate power. Or maybe my access to a wide network of others allows me to be influential through connectional power. Critically, the way I use my combined sources of power and influence determines how I am perceived and experienced by others. When I get it right, I have access to the holy grail of influence – referent power!

According to French and Raven (1986), we each have six sources of personal power available to us. Our wise engagement with these can greatly enhance our influence over others. In no significant order, first we have reward power. One of the main reasons we work is for the money we need to conduct and enjoy our lives. So, a fair rate of pay for a fair day's work may be considered the basic expression of what is termed *extrinsic* reward power in organizations. Beyond this there are many forms of so-called *intrinsic* reward that range from a simple 'thank you' to the granting of increased responsibility and accountability. On a more subtle level, listening to someone, helping them solve a problem, acknowledging their broader contributions or concerns are all forms of intrinsic reward. In essence we're giving people our time and, when given in a good spirit, this is appreciated. Thus, extrinsic rewards are to do with physical returns on our investment in work and intrinsic rewards are to do with psychological returns on our investment. But, as with all sources of power, there are negative forms of expression available. For example, the negative use of reward power may take the form of bribery or favouritism.

Next, we have *coercive power*. This is the power to make someone do something against their will. Within organizations, grievance and disciplinary practices are the obvious 'legitimate' embodiment of coercive power. National and international laws and policing mechanisms form the broader base of coercive power within a society. Outside of these legitimate uses of coercive power are the informal uses that may result in bullying or social exclusion.

Third, we have *expert power*. When a person has the knowledge and skills that someone else requires, then they have expert power. This is a very common form of power and is the basis for a large proportion of human collaboration, particularly within organizational life. The negative use of expert power may result in belittlement or one-upmanship.

Our fourth source of power is *legitimate power*, i.e. that which is invested in a specific role. Directors, managers, health and safety officers, all have legitimate power. This legitimacy may come from a higher source of power and is often linked with coercive power. A common trap that people may fall into regarding their legitimate power is to forget that people are obeying the position, not them. When they either fall from power or move on to other things, it can be a surprise that people who used to respond to their orders no longer do so! Beyond organizational life, we all have the legitimate power associated with living in a civilized society. This power is embodied within European and international laws regarding human rights. Occasionally, these rights are used to challenge the inappropriate use of coercive power within organizations. The negative use of legitimate power may be expressed as professional preciousness, inappropriate 'working to rule', or the classic 'jobsworth' attitude.

Next, we have *referent power*. This is the power a person gains from another person liking them, wanting to be like them, or seeing them as a role model for some aspect of their behaviour. At its extremes, it is the power of charisma and fame and is wielded by celebrities and local social leaders. Those with referent power can also use it for coercion. One of the things we fear most is social exclusion, and all it takes is a word from a social leader for us to be shunned by others in the group.

Last but not least we have *connectional power*. The degree to which we are 'well connected' within our highly networked world can have a major impact on our ability to influence individuals and formal or informal work groups. Highly connected individuals have power by virtue of the degree to which they can mobilize others (the 'bandwagon' effect). If the mobilization of others is in the direction of organizational aims, we see the positive side of connectional power. If mobilization is in opposition to organizational aims, we have the negative expression of connectional power.

Typically, managers gain four types of power upon appointment – the legitimate power of their position, the expert power that led to their appointment, reward power in the form of pay and reward strategies, and coercive power in the form of disciplinary procedures. However, the most valuable source of power for a manager, referent power, must be earned through the manager's efforts to act with a high degree of professional integrity. Credibility in a non-leadership role (i.e. prior to promotion or appointment) may carry over into the new role, but it is not a 'given'.

The key to using our sources of power successfully is to:

- Be sensitive to our sources of power and be consistent in their application to others

- Recognize the costs, risks and benefits of the different sources of power and draw on whichever is appropriate to the situation and person at hand

- Appreciate the value and dynamics of each source of power when it is applied appropriately

- Act maturely and exercise self-control, avoiding impulses and egotistical displays

- Understand that power is necessary to get things done.

All of the players in our story have all six sources of power available to them. However, the degrees to which they use their powers is highly variable. Examples from three of our characters are illustrated in the following table. Please read down each column in turn.

Sources of power/ influence	Manager	Payne	Jayne
Reward	The manager showed an initial interest in her team members' views …	No use of reward power was evidenced by Payne.	Jayne welcomed the operational change, but …
Legitimate	… and legitimately explored and introduced change, but …	Payne had the right to question the introduction of the new mallets, but …	… withdrew when her beliefs were compromised.
Coercive	… lost her person-centred approach and forced change.	… used professional preciousness to block change …	Jayne did not evidence any use of coercive power …
Expert	She did, however, use her expertise to focus on appropriate change and …	… then used his expertise as a weapon against change, citing …	… nor expert power …
Connectional	… used her Tunbridge Wells connection to enhance this expertise …	… his ancestral pedigree as a stonemason.	… nor connectional power, but …
Referent	… thereby gaining credibility with the Board of Trustees.	Payne would have referent power over other traditionalists.	… she might have become a role model for like-minded colleagues.

Figure 20: A summary of uses of power within the Gaudi scenario

As can be seen from Figure 20, our uses of power can be complex and either direct or indirect (see Force, where direct and indirect forms of resistance are explored).

 Effective managers use all six sources of power available to them in their 'positive' form. Using the template suggested in Figure 21 as a guide, consider your current uses of power and identify improvements you might target. Thereafter, you could self-coach around the identified improvements (see Coach).

Sources of power/ influence	How I apply it with ...			
	Team members	Peers	Line manager	Customers
Reward				
Legitimate				
Coercive				
Expert				
Connectional				
Referent				

Figure 21: Analysing own uses of power

Following this initial exercise you may find value in repeating the task at a greater level of detail, i.e. look at your application of power with each individual team member, peer and customer.

 To expand on some of the ideas discussed here, see Coach, Force, Lead, Motivation and Relationship.

Q

Being able to ask the right **question** is much more valuable than providing a mediocre answer.

Question

Question *n*. A form of words addressed to a person in order to elicit information.

Cliff, a friend and professional colleague of mine, developed the equation BQ + BA = BC (better questions plus better answers make for better choices). I share his view. But formulating a good (better!) question is not easy. As I reflect back on some of my most challenging assignments as an organization development consultant I recognize that part of what made these assignments so challenging was that I hadn't identified soon enough the real questions that the client and I were seeking to answer. For example, the client question 'How do I get my junior managers to take more responsibility for the quality of their work?' generated an organization development design that involved interviewing lots of junior managers, the delivery of quality improvement sessions and the review of some key operating procedures. All of this brought about a marginal improvement. But then, after reflecting on the many comments I'd heard, I was driven to ask the commissioning senior manager (who was also the line manager of many of the aberrant staff) 'What things might you have done, and might you still be doing, that would cause your staff to underperform in the way they do?' On coaching the manager towards an honest response, the solution to the problem became remarkably obvious – in principle at least. The manager was using an extremely directive style with his highly able, experienced and once motivated staff (see Lead). So it was that in the early days of my business consultancy practices I took pride in always having an answer. Now I realize that, in our complex and rapidly changing world, answers have a very short shelf life. Being able to ask the right question is much more valuable than providing a mediocre answer. Furthermore, in my practice as an executive coach, one of my most important tasks is to ask questions that cause my clients to consider possibilities they have not yet explored. Asking relevant questions of my clients provides them with new perspectives and insights into their actions and decisions, thus empowering them to see for themselves what is functional and what is dysfunctional in their decisions and behaviours.

A key and often ignored communication skill is that of asking good questions. A good question is one that is thought-provoking, open-ended and doesn't lead to a predetermined outcome, i.e. is not a 'leading question'. An effective question is not a 'why' question, but rather a 'what', 'how' or 'when' question. 'Why' questions are good for soliciting information, but can make people defensive, i.e. feel they have to justify themselves. So we must be thoughtful in our use of 'Why?' And critically, once we have asked an effective question we must then have the ability and patience to listen to the answer rather than provide it! Our ability to suspend judgement is also important. This is about wanting to understand what a person is really saying, i.e. what is behind their words. This requires us to let go of our opinions for a while so that they do not block us from learning.

Figure 22 shows examples of good questions that can help us improve our communication with, and understanding of, our colleagues and the situations they encounter.

Finally, here's a parting question for you to ponder: 'What could you gain by regularly asking your staff appropriate questions?'

(a) Questions aimed at clarifying an issue:	(c) Questions aimed at getting further information:
What seems to be the problem?	What do you mean by … ?
How do you feel about … ?	Tell me more about …
What concerns you the most about … ?	What have you tried so far?
What is holding you back from … ?	What have you achieved so far?
(b) Questions aimed at exploring outcomes:	(d) Questions aimed at taking action:
How do you want X to turn out?	What's your plan?
What do you want to achieve regarding X?	What will you do?
What benefits would you like to get out of X?	When will you do it?
If you do X, how will it affect Y and Z?	What else do you need to consider?

Figure 22: Some examples of effective questions

Let's try out some effective questions on the people working on the Gaudi Cathedral building project. When Wayne first met his new manager and gave his final response, 'And I do that all day', the manager might have asked, quite simply, 'And how do you feel about that?' Wayne would then have been required to acknowledge his negativity, allowing the manager to begin the process, from day one, of addressing the underlying issues that were causing not only the poor attitude, but also the unacceptable sickness absence record. Depending on how the conversation went, other effective questions may have included 'Tell me more about the time you've spent working on this project', 'What do you want to achieve regarding your work here?' or 'What do you want to get out of your job?'

With Payne, the manager did not address the issue of quality of workmanship in relation to productivity. Effective questions here might include (and we begin with the simplest) 'What's holding you back from producing ten blocks a day?' Again, depending on how the conversation went, other effective questions may have included 'What concerns you most about the accuracy of your work?', 'What will you have to do to achieve your productivity targets?', 'What do *you* want to achieve regarding the accuracy/productivity balance?' or 'If you achieve your productivity targets how will this affect your accuracy (and how do you feel about that)?'

With regard to Sayne's response to the manager's introductory statement, 'I'm finding out what you all do', with Sayne's answer being 'I'm a member of the stonemasonry team', the manager could have then asked 'And how do you find working in the team?' This may have revealed all manner of early insights.

In response to her cool reaction to the news about the new arts and performance centre, Jayne might have benefited from being asked 'What concerns you most about this change in direction?', and beyond this, questions such as 'Tell me more about what motivates you so highly in your job', 'What benefits would you get out of being a part of this new direction?' and 'If you complete this project, how will it affect your other aspirations?'

Approaching her team with this questioning style would certainly have provided the manager with more quality information with which to build her working relationships and hence improve her ability to create the conditions in which her team members could feel most motivated. You might wish to ponder what questions, from those listed above, could have been asked of Wayne, Payne, Jayne and the Board of Trustees at other points in the story.

This exercise is simple. Take the time to ask some good questions – and be curious enough to truly listen to the answers. As a primer to this, you might select a range of recent interchanges with colleagues that have left you feeling dissatisfied. With the wisdom of hindsight, what questions might you have asked? Beyond these reflections, what opportunities might you develop to ask questions in the near future? What might these questions be targeted towards, i.e. clarifying an issue, exploring outcomes, getting further information or taking action? Maybe use the questions listed in Figure 22 to guide your approach.

It is important to adopt a non-threatening stance/attitude when asking questions. Be curious instead. Hopefully this will be how you feel anyway. Seek first to understand, before you seek to be understood!

Appropriate links to ideas discussed here can be found under Coach, Force, Habit, Relationship and Walkabout.

R

What determines the quality and longevity of our **relationship**s is how we deal with renegotiations.

Relationship

Relationship *n.* A connection between people.

As a youngster, I found that developing, maintaining and ending relationships was both a natural and relatively simple part of my social life. Those around me said what they thought and asked for what they needed in plain, straightforward terms. I didn't always like what I heard, but at least I knew where I stood. And I had clear feedback that enabled me to adapt my behaviour if a relationship was important to me. But as I progressed through youth and into adulthood things changed. Relationships became much more complex. I now live in a world where many of my relationships are confused by a lack of simple clarity, hidden agendas, 'spun' messages and subconscious sensitivities. Because of this, I have to reflect on exchanges, deal with ambiguity, second-guess others' likely reactions and generally apply more energy to the process of maintaining effective relationships. I have to be alert to the nuances of exchanges and be equally aware of what isn't being said.

Given all of this, the light started to shine on my relationships when I stumbled, in the mid-1980s, across a paper written by Sherwood and Glidewell (1973). The paper describes a model that we can use to appreciate, in real time, what is going on in a relationship. Since taking this model on board most of my relationships have returned to their earlier healthy state. I say 'most' because it takes two to tango!

When we develop a relationship of any kind, the first step involves us in sharing information about who we are, what we're interested in, our aspirations, our (good) habits, etc. From these initial exchanges of information we start to build expectations. If the relationship is tied in with employment or the membership of a formal group we will negotiate some of these expectations explicitly and in detail. But for informal relationships much of the negotiation is covert and not stated formally. If we hear enough of what we want to hear during our initial exchanges we make a commitment. But this commitment is usually clouded by many factors, the most significant of which is that in these early stages we tend to tell the other person what we think they want to hear. So, the initial expectations we have of each other are often flawed. And from this basis we move into a period of relative stability and productivity.

Then comes the first inevitable pinch. Inevitable because all relationships are dynamic and require continual renegotiation. Even if initial expectations are fully shared and based on full and accurate information (which is highly unlikely), changes occur over time. These changes may be due to changing circumstances for the individuals involved in the relationship, a changing context in which the relationship exists, or the surfacing of expectations that were not originally shared. What determines the quality and longevity of our relationships is how we deal with renegotiations.

The model illustrated in Figure 23, based on the work of Sherwood and Glidewell, provides a simple and effective way of understanding the dynamics of our relationships. It also highlights the importance of addressing issues before the undesirable consequences of shifting expectations take too large a toll.

When changes in expectations or circumstances are not addressed at an early stage (i.e. when they are left to go beyond the 'pinch'), they may bring about severe disruptions to the relationship, as anyone who has experienced a 'crunch' will know. Crunches are often characterized by arguments, a lack of constructive or meaningful communication and growing feelings of anxiety. Alternatively, some of us may hold our feelings in and store them up for action at a later date. Either way, once the immediacy of a crunch has passed, what often happens is that the people involved in the relationship return to the way things were just prior to the crunch. Apologies may be exchanged, conflicts smoothed over and a renewed but shaky commitment returns. Further 'crunches' inevitably follow and the partners in the relationship thereafter become ever more deeply unsatisfied. Eventually, withdrawal becomes the only coping mechanism. This withdrawal is psychological at first, but then manifests as a physical withdrawal, i.e. spending less time 'in' the relationship, missing meetings, taking sickness absence, etc.

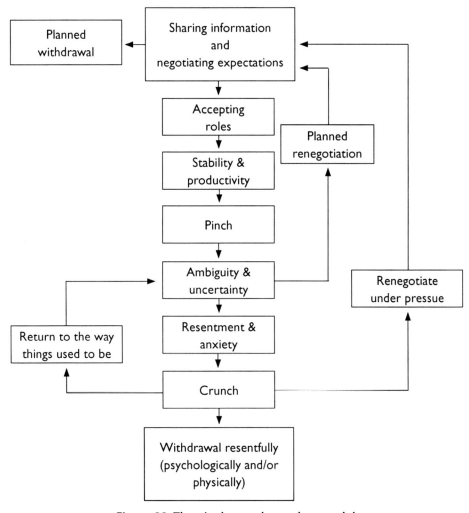

Figure 23: The pinches and crunches model

Fortunately this pattern of events is not inevitable. There is a way of effectively managing the dynamics of relationships. If, on feeling a pinch, we cycle back to the starting point and share any new information that has become apparent or available, we can engage in a planned and timely renegotiation of expectations without the interference of a high emotional charge. A new set of shared expectations can be established and revised roles can be accepted on the basis of this review and renewal session. If new expectations cannot be agreed, withdrawal is still available, but in this case it can be agreed upon rather than being a unilateral decision based on untested assumptions. Unfortunately, there is a natural tendency for us to ignore early warning signs in relationships (i.e. pinches). Overcoming this tendency is probably the most significant improvement we can make to both our personal relationships and to our leadership and management styles.

Our behaviour in the first ten seconds or so of contact with a new working colleague will make a lasting impression on them. With Wayne, the manager's first impression of negativity was confirmed in subsequent interactions. Wayne had withdrawn from his job. With Payne, the first impression was one of a professional who really cared about doing a good job. But in reality, his interest was in doing just one aspect of a good job – and overdoing it at that. An over-intensive focus on the size tolerances of his building blocks at the expense of meeting productivity targets was initially masked, but revealed itself after a few weeks of monitoring. This created a pinch for the new manager. However, by then she had become excited about introducing a new style of mallet and so failed to address the pinch caused by Payne's unbalanced performance focus. Without doubt, this would have been a difficult issue to address with Payne as he saw his identity as being that of a master stonemason and his expression of his identity was in the accuracy with which he reproduced building blocks. Beyond this, the manager perpetuated Payne's inappropriate performance through her response to his unexpected positive reaction to the change of strategic direction of the project (cathedral to arts centre).

In contrast with Payne, Jayne expressed her commitment to the building of the cathedral by producing 15 blocks a day. But a third of these blocks fell outside the required size tolerances. As with Payne, the new manager failed to get on top of this issue. So pinches were well on the path to becoming crunches – crunches that would most likely be expressed when it was time for the annual performance reviews that would determine pay increases. However, things moved rather more quickly than that. Both Payne and Jayne kept silent about their growing feelings of anxiety and resentment. Payne's anxiety and resentment were caused by the introduction of the new mallets. Jayne's were caused by the change in strategic direction, from cathedral to theatre and arts centre. Both Payne and Jayne passed through the pinch stage into unexpressed crunches, as evidenced by their 'surprise' physical withdrawals when both chose to leave the organization on the same day.

The manager's first impression of Sayne must have been one of him being well-adjusted to his job and his working environment. And as the story progressed this first impression was reinforced, making it easy for the manager to take him for granted, i.e. not give him the positive attention he deserved.

If we have a real desire to develop and maintain fully functional relationships, it is important that we take the time to develop the level of trust and understanding necessary to address pinches before they become crunches. In many organizations, regular one-to-one meetings provide an appropriate context for this, assuming these meetings are conducted well. One-to-ones should be held at intervals that take account of how quickly pinches can become crunches. Two factors determine this interval: the work itself and the characteristics of the individuals doing the work.

The following exercise will help you and your team explore the relationships model and create a more open and productive environment for relationships to flourish.

1. Explain the relationship model to your team.

2. Identify some crunches you have experienced in the past year or so.

3. Using the relationships model, discuss how one of these crunches developed, from the initial pinch, through the build-up of ambiguity and uncertainty, to become a situation where anxiety and resentment led into the crunch.

4. If the crunch was not effectively addressed, i.e. there was no effective renegotiation, explore what did happen.

5. Identify the early warning signs that may have led you to address the issue at the pinch stage.

6. Identify the barriers that prevented you from addressing the pinch.

7. Draw some lessons from the exercise, i.e. a new set of ground rules for how you will act in the future.

If you have any energy left after carrying out steps 1 to 7 above, there are two further options.

1. Explore a second crunch, i.e. repeat steps 3 to 7.

2. Identify some current pinches and address them now, i.e. before they become crunches, using the new ground rules developed in step 7 above.

 To expand on some of the ideas discussed here, see also Aspiration, Involvement, Motivation, Transition and Zen.

S

Scenarios can help us attune to, recognize and adapt in real time to changing environmental conditions.

Scenario

Scenario *n.* A potential sequence of events expressed as a narrative or story.

Any time I think about the future I'm creating a scenario, i.e. a story about how things might be. By imagining what might change and what I might do about it I can position myself to minimize threats and take advantage of opportunities. Critically, I don't begin creating my scenarios with a completely blank page. If I did, the task of thinking about the future would be overwhelming. Rather, there is at least one thing I know with complete certainty: I know my life is finite. Beyond this (dramatic) certainty there are other things that I know with a significant degree of certainty. For example, information and communications technologies will continue to have a growing impact on how I experience and live my life. And I am likely to find my children challenging during their teenage years. Beyond these relative certainties are other things that are quite uncertain. Will I continue to engage in enjoyable and profitable work? Will our family investments blossom or wither? When faced with such uncertainties I develop contingency plans in order to reduce risk and/or enhance my abilities to take advantage of opportunities. I have found that the more structured and thorough I am in my contingency planning, the more likely I am to thrive, regardless of what the future holds – within obvious limits!

Within organizational life there are two broad approaches to using scenarios. The traditional way is to develop a story of the future with a high reliance on quantitative data. This typically results in a clear prediction accompanied by a sensitivity analysis that offers variations around this prediction – the so-called econometric model. The problem with this approach is that econometric models, despite growing sophistication, are always prone to the 'butterfly effect' as described by Gleick (1998). Consequently, an alternative approach was developed in the 1970s through the work of Pierre Wack, a strategic planner with Royal Dutch/Shell. Through his early efforts, Shell adopted a now celebrated approach to scenario planning supported by dedicated, short-term (two year), virtual teams.

For Shell, scenarios become stories about the way the world might turn out at some specified point in the future. This approach can help us attune to, recognize and adapt in real time to changing environmental conditions (see External). A law of ecology states that for an organism (animal or plant) to survive, its rate of adaptation must be as fast as the rate of change of its environment. Taking dinosaurs as a well-cited example, the catastrophic and rapid changes to the Earth's environment around 65 million years ago brought about their extinction because they were unable to evolve 'in the moment'. Prior to that, they had thrived through gradual evolution for some 165 million years. To date, humans have lived on planet Earth for a little over one million years (a humbling thought, I think). By adapting the ecological law just a little, we have a highly poignant guideline for modern organizations. For an organization to thrive, its rate of adaptation must be at least as fast as the rate of change in its environment. I say 'at least as fast' as it is conceivable that, with our increasingly subtle abilities to model the world, we may have the tools to shape aspects of our operating environments and so be ahead of the changes.

Through a scenario-planning process leaders can invent and then consider in depth several varied stories of equally plausible futures. If these stories are carefully researched and include all relevant details, they may give rise to flashes of insight and unexpected leaps in understanding. This helps us prepare for the future because the point is not to pick one preferred scenario and hope for it to come to pass (tempting though this might be if we're aiming to satisfy our inherent desires for certainty), but to make strategic decisions that will be sound for a wide range of plausible futures. Thereafter, regardless of what future actually arises, we are much more likely to be ready for it, adapt to it and maybe play a role in shaping it.

Back in the late 19th century, Antoni Gaudi had a clear scenario in mind as he worked on the Sagrada Familia. His scenario was based on assumptions he held about the future of belief and behaviour in Barcelona, Spain and the world at large. His cathedral was going to be the largest structure in the Christian world and we can reasonably assume that his scenario included a growing number of practising Christians in Barcelona such that the cathedral would be a thriving and active community that didn't threaten the existence of the established parish churches. Indeed, Gaudi may have seen his project as being at the forefront of meeting the future needs of a rapidly growing city. However, and through the fortuitous insights of the new construction manager, this scenario was eventually challenged in the light of the social and economic changes that had taken place in the intervening century since the project began. But that, as they say, is history.

The point to consider now is the degree to which the new manager may have fallen into a similar trap to that which caught Gaudi, i.e. will the new manager's scenario of cultural tourism and an increasingly secular global community prove to be any more robust over the next hundred years than Gaudi's scenario of a growing Christian population has been over the last hundred? Certainly, the manager presented a compelling case based on today's realities and trends. But that's just what Gaudi did. What might be the alternative future scenarios over, say, the next 25 years?

Two key assumptions in the new manager's scenario were increased cultural tourism and a continuing decline in the use of churches as expressions of faith. Maybe we could call this scenario the 'Secular Global Village'. If we make some alternative assumptions we could come up with an entirely different scenario which we could call 'Religious and Cultural Isolationism'. In this scenario, climate change and the actions of the major oil-producing nations drive the price of oil-based fuels to unimaginable highs, thus making international air travel fall back to the levels of the 1950s. Furthermore, in this scenario, the decline in the population of practising Christians is significantly reversed as a cultural competitive response to the expansion of non-Christian faiths and secularism. And developments in information and communications technologies advance far enough to offer credible virtual reality experiences that captivate the new generation (born in the first decade of the 21st century). Cultural tourism is replaced by 'cultural immersion' as the twenty-somethings of 2030 embrace virtual reality experiences that put them *into* the visual and performing arts rather than restrict them to the role of an *observer* of the arts.

Clearly, the new manager's strategy for the development of an arts and performance centre scores highly in the Secular Global Village scenario. But it rapidly becomes a white elephant in the Religious and Cultural Isolationism scenario. So what would a robust strategy for the next 25 years look like? I leave you, the reader, to think about this should you have the inclination. And I hope you do, as it would be a valuable primer for the team exercise that follows. By way of a hint, you might explore York Minster for starters!

Although those organizations that have benefited most from the scenario approach to planning and decision making are the ones who have invested in dedicated scenario-planning functions, I have worked with many organizations that have still gained significant value from a scenario approach to planning based on a more modest scale of organization and activity. The exercise that follows can be completed with just four or five days' effort expended over a period of a month or two.

1. First select your scenario planning team. Ideally this will include representation from all of the functions within your team or organization. You may also include selected experts from outside (a purely internal team will rarely be able to achieve breakthrough thinking).

2. Bring the scenario team together and introduce the concept of scenario planning. A Google search will provide additional resources to those included here.

3.   Select the appropriate time horizon for your scenarios. This will depend on the nature of your organization's business and the characteristics of the environment it populates. An oil company such as Shell may adopt a twenty-year horizon. A telecommunications company such as Orange may adopt a five-year horizon. Factors such as maturity of the industry, rate of technological change, environmental pressures and the organization's competitive position will all have an influence on the time horizon you adopt. Explore these issues with your scenario team.

4.   Look at the present and the past. Before you can use scenarios to look ahead, you need to develop a shared understanding of how your organization has acted in the past and the current situation in which it now finds itself. Start by asking:

   •   Where have we been (how has the organization evolved to date)?
   •   What have we done (how have we dealt with change and how do we innovate)?
   •   Where are we now (how are we positioned and what are the current visible trends)?

5.   Develop a pool of scenarios. Although a large meeting involving all the key players is the best way of starting a scenario-planning effort, the use of subgroups is often the best way of conducting the preliminary scenario development work. So, create two or more subgroups from your scenario team (between three and five members per group). Each group should now develop two scenarios to feed back to the full scenario team. The process for developing the scenarios within the subgroups is as follows:

   (a) Use STEEPLE analysis (see External) to identify evolutionary trends and possible major developments that could occur in your operating environment. Remember to link this analysis to the time horizon identified in step 3 above.

   (b) Separate the factors identified in step (a) into one group containing relatively certain developments or trends, and another group containing relatively uncertain developments or trends (i.e. those that might go one way or another).

(c) Divide the relatively uncertain developments or trends into two further groups. When doing this it might make sense to group some uncertainties together as there may appear to be a logical way of clustering them, i.e. there is a likelihood that they would occur within the same scenario. For example, within a single national economy high interest rates are often associated with high exchange rates and reduced demand for exports.

(d) Place one set of relative uncertainties onto one flipchart sheet and the other set onto a second sheet.

(e) Add the relative certainties to both flipchart sheets – both scenarios will have these elements in common.

(f) Develop the scenario logics and narratives, i.e. tell the story of the scenario (see Narrative). Make this story as vivid and imaginative as possible – but maintain a sensible degree of reality. And give each of the scenarios a distinctive and memorable name (e.g. Next Wave, Ripples on Sand, Secular Global Village, Divided World, Life on a Chip).

(g) Flesh out the scenarios. Once the basic scenarios have been established, explore other trends or developments that might be used to enrich your narratives.

6. Now the scenarios have been developed and the narratives have been written within the subgroups, it is time to reconvene the full scenario team and share outputs in the style of a *'scenario conference'*. Presentations can be made, similarities and differences between the scenarios explored, and a decision made regarding which two or three scenarios will be adopted for the next stage of the exercise. These scenarios can be finalized, i.e. written up in a consistent style and with comparable levels of detail.

7. The next step is to generate a range of strategic options for the organization (see Option and Unique). Such options should be generated in a non-judgemental environment, i.e. all suggestions are initially accepted for the sake of injecting further creativity into the exercise. They can be refined later.

8. Test each option by asking 'How does this option fare in each of our agreed scenarios?'; 'What vulnerabilities are revealed?'; 'Is the decision robust across all scenarios or does it look good in just one

scenario?' If a decision looks good in only one scenario, then it qualifies as a high-risk gamble. The question then might be 'How could that decision be adapted to make it more robust across a range of our scenarios?'

9.   On the basis of step 8, work towards establishing the favoured strategic options for your team or organization. Thereafter, develop the appropriate action plan for implementation.

10. Finally, let the art of the strategic conversation flourish. As people become familiar with the names and details of your chosen scenarios, increasingly they may feature in general conversations. For example, it will be enough to say *'In the Secular Global Village scenario, purchasing this resource presents us with a very shaky investment'*, or *'In the Next Wave scenario, we'd gain a great competitive advantage from purchasing rather than leasing this resource'*. Conversations like this can add enormous benefit to the opportunities your organization has to thrive.

For the exercise outlined above I have drawn on the work of Peter Schwartz (1996).

As discussed in the Introduction, stories offer us a means to see and understand our individual worlds in new and enlightened ways. New insights become possible as we reframe our experiences within scenarios that strip away irrelevant, confusing or emotive details. Our perceptual filters of convenience or defence are lifted and we can explore previously unseen avenues of analysis and action. Stories can help us generate creativity and greater choice. Herein lies the power and value of a scenario approach to medium- and long-term planning.

To expand on some of the ideas discussed here, see Aspiration, External, Narrative, Option and Unique.

T

 It is not the change we manage, it is the **transition**s that we and those around us undergo that are managed.

Transition

Transition *n.* The period of time during which something changes.

 'Change' seems to have gained a bad name in modern western culture. I believe the reasons for this are many and varied and during my reflections I find it helpful to place change into two categories: those changes which I initiate and towards which I have a positive approach, and those changes initiated by others and towards which I may have a positive or negative approach. The key determinant of my approach in this latter case is how I perceive the potential costs and benefits to me as an individual. Will the cost of the change be outweighed by the benefits of the change to me personally? But then a complication arises. My perceptions of costs and benefits tend to change as change itself progresses. Changes I initiated myself because I initially saw a good cost–benefit balance may cost more than I originally estimated (or the benefits I anticipated don't amount to quite so much). And the opposite can be true for change initiated by others – costs turn out to be less and benefits more. Having children fell, temporarily, into the first category; restructuring my business based on the demands of a client fell into the latter.

Much is written about change; much is said about change; little changes about change! Change is still as poorly managed in 21st-century organizations as it was in the last century. This is because few people understand the dynamics of change or have the emotional intelligence to engage with change productively. Here we will consider the transitional aspects of change because it is in this detail that the devil resides!

When change happens it is not the change we manage, it is the transitions that we and those around us undergo that are managed. In other words, we don't manage change; we manage the transitions of ourselves and others. Figure 24 illustrates three intuitive and well-documented phases that people pass through when confronted by change, i.e. endings, the neutral zone and new beginnings. Let's look at these in more detail.

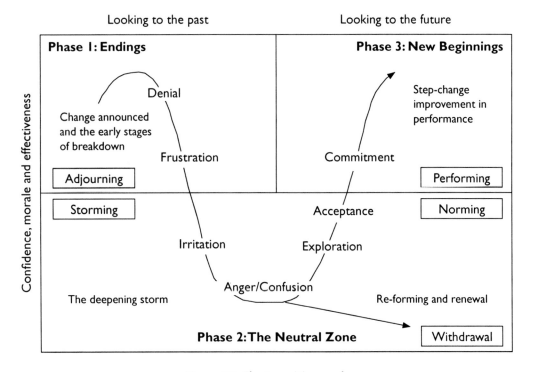

Figure 24: The transition cycle

When change is announced, usually at a time when people feel they have just recovered from the last change and are looking forward to a period of stability, the change is typically denied – people appear not to 'hear' what's going on. This is largely because they don't want to hear. However, as they are compelled to hear, frustration develops when they begin to engage with the evolving situation. Resistance develops, signalled by statements about the naivety of managers and the madness of the change. People then move into the neutral zone where it becomes clear that they are being pressured to let go of current structures, systems and ways of doing things in favour of *the new*, even though the new has not been tested or even made clear to them. It is at this stage that a range of real or imagined losses become apparent. Typically these losses relate to issues of status, power, relationships and security. The experience of these losses cause the irritation, anger and confusion that are so often evident during transitions.

The true transition point is reached when anger, the lowest part of the curve, evolves into confusion. At this stage, the focus of people's attention moves from the past to the future. They are confused about what this change is going to mean to them and how they need to react. They stop making statements that refer back to some ideal past (that never really existed) and start asking questions about the future. Exploration, acceptance and commitment eventually move people into a new status quo where intended increases or realignments in performance take place – prior to further change! It is usual within an organization that some people will not make it through some transitions. At the anger/confusion boundary, withdrawal may occur – initially psychological and then physical (see Relationship for a fuller treatment of this process).

Because of a continuing prevalence of naive management styles in the workplace, most change management strategies are doomed to failure from the start. Many people's style of managing change can be likened to gardeners standing over their plants imploring them to grow. 'Try harder!' 'You can do it!' In the words of Senge (1999), no gardener tries to convince a plant to 'want' to grow. If the seed does not have the potential to grow, there's nothing anyone can do to make a difference. Effective change leadership strategies focus on understanding the limiting processes that could slow or block change. Above all else, effective gardeners understand the constraints that can limit growth, and then they attend to those constraints. If information and support are available and people are able to maintain a sense of meaning and control, they will pass through the lower parts of the transition curve and develop a future-oriented perspective which engages them in exploration and an eventual commitment to change.

On the basis of Wayne's upfront negativity on the new manager's arrival, we can surmise that he had almost certainly suffered frustration, irritation and anger, which had led to his clear withdrawal from both his job and the building project as a whole. But, in this case, his withdrawal is only psychological, i.e. he still turned up for work, most of the time. His behaviour may be evidence of his experience of one too many changes that were handled poorly. Moving on to Payne, he was jogging along quite nicely prior to the new manager's arrival. But then, with the introduction of the new mallet, he never moved further than 'anger'. He didn't express this anger openly, but his silent psychological withdrawal eventually became a total physical withdrawal when he resigned. Sayne remained sanguine. But for how long would he tolerate his manager's refusal to engage with his interest in being more involved? Jayne moved rapidly round the curve to commitment on the issue of the mallet but on the issue of the change of use for the building she withdrew. What the manager failed to do with her team members was to understand their personal motivations and support them on an individual basis. Treating them all as the individuals they clearly were would have helped them each make sense of the changes in their own terms. The section on Motivation covers this in greater depth.

Having the knowledge and ability to manage transitions is possibly the most important attribute for an effective leader in the 21st century. This is for two reasons. First, change is happening at an ever-increasing rate so there are a lot of transitions to be managed. Second, younger generations of employees are questioning more rigorously the fit they feel between themselves and their employing organizations. The following exercise may be a useful way of exploring the issues of change and transition facing you and your team.

Identify a specific change your team has recently experienced and ask yourselves, within the context of a development day or team meeting, the following questions (refer back to 'Notes on the practical exercises' if necessary):

1. With reference to the change we are exploring, what did we say and do when we were first confronted with the change, i.e. how did we acknowledge this position when we were in the 'Endings' part of the transition curve?

2.   What did we say and do when we were working through the most difficult stages of the transition, i.e. when we were in the 'Neutral' part of the transition curve, experiencing irritation and anger?

3.   What did we say and do once we had passed the lowest part of the transition curve and were moving towards 'New Beginnings', i.e. what questions did we ask and what options did we explore?

4.   What losses did we experience or fear? (In the first instance this question could be answered as an individual exercise using the table in Figure 25 as a guide.)

5.   What have we learned from this exercise that will help us better manage transitions in the future?

	Potential or actual losses that may be experienced ...			
	... by me	... by others in the team	... by the team as a whole	Actions I/we took
Status				
Power/influence				
Relationships				
Personal future				
Sense of competence				
Sense of control				
Identity				

Figure 25: An analysis of team and individual losses associated with change

Finally, a table similar to Figure 25 could be used when a new change is on the horizon. Proactively completing this exercise during the 'frustration' stage of the transition may contribute significantly to an effective change strategy for your team.

 To expand on some of the ideas discussed here, see also Aspiration, Involve, Motivation, Question and Relationship.

U

Every business should have a value proposition that makes it **unique**.

Unique

Unique *adj*. Being the only one of a particular type.

'He'll never be a David Attenborough!' That's what my mother and father were told on a parents' evening at my school when I was about fourteen years old. When I heard this I remember saying in a highly irritated tone that I didn't want to be a 'David Attenborough' anyway. I wanted to be a 'Carl Taylor'. As I look back on this incident (which clearly had a profound effect on me!) I know that my first reaction all those years ago was in no small part a rebellious one. But I still hold on to the sentiment. David Attenborough has spent his life doing his 'David Attenborough' thing uniquely. And I'm spending my life doing my 'Carl Taylor' thing uniquely. We each have our own USP (unique selling proposition). My USP has enabled me to secure a range of jobs and partners in the face of occasionally fierce competition. I've also lost out a few times to people with stronger USPs.

As the journey continues, my strategy has been to focus my greatest efforts on exploiting my natural strengths. This is a strategy explored well by Buckingham and Clifton (2004). They argue that to excel in your chosen field, and find satisfaction in doing so, you need to become an expert in understanding, applying and refining your unique strengths.

 No organization can be all things to all people, so each tends naturally to differentiate itself on some particular attribute that will give it an advantage over the competition. Treacy and Wiersema (1996) developed the so-called 'value disciplines model' to help explain and assist in the development of differentiation strategies. They argued that every business should have a value proposition that makes it unique and this needs to be supported by an appropriate operating model. They further argued that, in essence, there are just three generic value propositions:

- Operational excellence – pursuing the best cost position. This is displayed by 'solid' companies such as BHS, FedEx and Kia Motors. These companies offer relatively high quality at a relatively low price. They tend not to think up new products and services, but rather they observe the market's direction and execute well those activities that have proven successful. The focus is on efficiency, cost and streamlining.

- Product leadership – offering the best product and being the first to do so. This is displayed by inventors and brand marketers such as Sony, Intel and Nike. They constantly experiment with new products, services and experiences. Margins are high because of the high risks involved in this strategy. The focus is on development, design and time to market.

- Customer intimacy – being the most dependable and responsive to customer needs. This is displayed by those who focus most energetically on keeping their customers happy and building an enduring relationship, e.g. Wexas Travel, Amazon and Rolls-Royce. These companies don't believe in one-time transactions. They invest time and money in their customers. They want to know everything about their customers and work in partnership with them. The focus is on customer relationships, exceeding expectations and customer retention.

Although combinations of these three generic disciplines are possible, pursuing more than one can lead to confusion and internal conflict, causing energy to be wasted. The best approach is to focus on one discipline – but choose it very carefully. Ideally it should be the one that has naturally emerged from the interplay of the organization's values, talents and workforce behaviours.

What was Antoni Gaudi's value proposition for the Sagrada Familia in the 19th century? From our opening story the answer appears to be primarily product leadership (the best cathedral in the world), closely followed by customer intimacy (providing the people of Barcelona with the means to celebrate their faith). Operational excellence, i.e. the pursuit of the best cost position, did not feature at all at this stage. However, operational excellence became a contributing factor with the arrival of the new manager and the introduction of sustainable construction methods.

The key to the Gaudi project's continuing success in the 21st century and beyond will be to devise and pursue an appropriate value proposition and operating model that will continue to be fit for purpose in the light of future trends. You, the reader, might contemplate this further. What do you think the appropriate value proposition will be? As with our exploration of Scenario, your reflections will be an excellent primer for the team exercise that follows.

This is a three-stage exercise. The first two stages can be completed within the same development session, or separated into two sessions a week or so apart. The third stage is likely to involve a subgroup of those who took part in Stages 1 and 2.

Stage 1 (1–2 hours required)

1.   Bring your team together and begin by describing the value discipline concept, using the preceding notes and your further internet-based research as resources.

2.   Place five sheets of flipchart paper around the walls, each with one of the questions below as its header:

    •   Which of the value disciplines means most to our current customers?

- Roughly how many customers, from the full base of all potential customers, focus on each type of value?
- What do our competitors focus on (name and be specific with regard to each key competitor)?
- Where do we stand within our competitive environment?
- What options for action do we have?

3. Ask team members to write their responses to each of these questions on large post-it notes and then stick them to the appropriate sheet on the wall. They can each produce more than one post-it per sheet. Indeed, encourage them to do so.

4. When everyone has run out of ideas, allocate a sheet to each individual (if five or fewer team members are taking part) or to small groups (if six or more are taking part) and ask them to review the post-its and develop a comprehensive and ordered summary on the appropriate flipchart sheet.

5. These summaries are then fed back to the full group and discussed.

6. Once all sheets have been covered, stand back and draw out themes and priorities. If time permits, carry on to Stage 2 of the exercise. If time is short, return as a group in the near future and continue.

Stage 2 (2–3 hours required)

1. Reflect fully on the outputs from Stage 1. Add further notes or comments if appropriate.

2. Now explore, in turn, what the adoption of each of the three value disciplines would mean for the team. The following questions might help:

What impact might adopting an operational excellence strategy (product leadership strategy/customer intimacy strategy) have on our:

(a) Operations
(b) Turnover
(c) Profitability
(d) Sustainability
(e) Competitive position
(f) Key stakeholders?

3. Once these questions have been answered for each of the three generic strategies, reflect on the output and review the relevance of the current value discipline you are operating.

4. If you determine that a new or enhanced approach to value discipline is required (and often the latter is true, if not the former) establish who will take part in Stage 3. This is likely to be a smaller, highly able and committed team that may include internal high performers and external experts.

5. Develop an outline project plan for Stage 3.

Stage 3 (10–20+ hours required as determined by the project plan)

1. The task is to determine, in detail, the following:

    - Operating models with design specifications for all key processes, systems, structures, etc.
    - Where the real value will lie in the new/revised strategy
    - The anticipated levels of additional value that may be achieved on the two value proposition dimensions that are not the primary focus of the proposed strategy
    - Projected revenues and profits
    - Key success factors and risk analyses
    - An audit against the organization's stated vision, mission and values
    - A transition plan for the next two to three years.

2. On completion of their analyses, this group should present their findings back to the full group, as originally convened for Stages 1 and 2.

3. Finally, senior management should decide the way forward.

This exercise could result in a major organizational effort as it may prompt a change of strategic focus. If there is reluctance on anyone's part to engage in this, there are three key questions that need to be answered before the effort is abandoned. These are:

1. If not this, what?
2. If not us, who?
3. If not now, when?

To expand on some of the ideas discussed here, see Aspiration, Balance, External, Scenario, Transition, Vision and Yield.

V

The leader's primary task is to create a shared **vision** for their team or organization.

Vision

Vision *n*. A vivid mental image produced by the imagination.

Eight years ago our family moved into a new housing development that had been built on the site of a former town centre school. Part of our decision to buy this particular house was the vision that was presented to us by the builder's agent. This took the form of an artist's impression of a mixed housing development with a play park, communal gardens and lots of open space to allow easy access to drives and garages. All of the 'off-plan' purchasers shared this vision of uncluttered community living. However, within a year of moving into our new homes our vision faded. Being positioned in the centre of town, and with no enforceable parking restrictions, much of our communal areas had become a free car park for office workers and shoppers. The residents who moved into the development after this situation had developed accepted the clutter of vehicles and its associated inconvenience as the norm. So, when proposals were put to the Residents Association for the introduction of road markings and a no-parking enforcement scheme that covered the communal areas there was a great deal of heated debate with a clear polarization between the early off-plan purchasers and the later purchasers who accepted, prior to purchase, the inconvenience of the parking situation. During a few tense meetings, the two opposing groups established firm and seemingly intractable positions – the 'visionaries' who wanted to achieve their vision of uncluttered and easy access to their drives and garages, and the 'realists' who accepted the reality of bumping their cars over the corners of front gardens and pavements to gain access to their drives. The turning point came when a resident presented the original artist's impression for the development along with a few photographs of the current state of affairs. Things changed rapidly after this. A consensus was reached on what people were willing to give up in order to attain the vision. We now live in a clutter-free, easy-access environment in the middle of town.

 Inspirational leadership begins with a vision, i.e. a clear and compelling view of how things could be. By establishing a vision you create something towards which others can direct their efforts. In essence, a shared vision helps unite people towards a purpose. So, the leader's primary task is to create a shared vision for their team or organization. However, the concepts of vision and mission are often misunderstood. A vision is an aspirational view of how the world could be. A mission is what an organization will do to contribute to the vision becoming a reality. Therefore, a successful vision can:

- Create a shared purpose

- Give a sense of the future

- Guide decision making and strategy

- Provide guidelines that determine behaviour

- Inspire emotion.

Dilts (1996) identified four key tasks for the visionary leader:

- Forming and clarifying a vision

- Sharing the vision with others

- Transforming the vision into actions (a mission)

- Engaging the help of others to fulfil the mission.

These tasks will form the foundation for the team exercise that follows, but first let's explore the relevance of vision to our Gaudi story.

Simply put, the vision statement of an organization should state clearly what the founder ultimately wants to achieve. Antoni Gaudi's vision was to create the finest structure in the Christian world where the people of Barcelona could celebrate their faith. In our opening story, both Wayne and Payne were preoccupied with the job in hand, i.e. stonemasonry, with no reference to the bigger vision to which they were contributing. Sayne presented himself as the team player who took a healthy interest in what was going on around him. Jayne was the torchbearer for Gaudi's original vision, having personalized its relevance to her own family for the next hundred generations! The new manager accepted her job on the project with Gaudi's vision clearly in mind. However, she adjusted the vision in the light of a hundred years of social evolution that had influenced the cathedral's original target market. Her revised vision, as alluded to at the meeting of the trustees, may have been expressed as follows:

> To build a world class arts and performance centre that will, through the sponsorship of local parish churches, enable the people of Barcelona to celebrate their faith.

This revised vision is consistent with the core values that underpinned Gaudi's original vision. But even though the trustees were convinced of this, Jayne was not. The critical issue regarding the manager's approach to Jayne was that she failed to make the link between the completion of the Gaudi Arts and Performance Centre and the sponsorship of the local parish churches. This failure was due to the poor quality of the manager's communications with Jayne. And because Jayne did not buy into the vision, she failed to buy into the case for change – a phenomenon explored further under Jam and Transition.

In the exercise that follows, we will work towards the development (or reaffirmation) of your team's vision, ensuring it conveys a compelling image of a desired future towards which you and your colleagues will make a contribution. Your vision should provide inspiration and challenge to all team members, assuming all are personally aligned with the organization (see Aspiration to explore this point further).

About two hours will be needed for this exercise.

1.   Bring your team members together and, following an introduction that draws on the notes above, ask them to independently imagine the best possible situation for the customers they serve in five to ten years' time. Allow a few minutes for this free flow of thoughts.

2.   Place six sheets of flipchart paper around the walls, each with one of the questions below as its header:

   (a)   Who are our target customers?

   (b)   Where are our target customers (our geographical scope)?

   (c)   What are the key products/services we currently offer?

   (d)   What will be the ideal situation for our customers in 5–10 years' time?

   (d)   What will be the key products/services we will offer in 5–10 years' time?

   (e)   How can we ensure we are offering the ideal for our customers in the future?

3.   Ask team members to write their responses to each question on large post-it notes and stick them to the appropriate sheet on the wall.

4.   When everyone has 'posted' their full set of responses, allocate a sheet to each individual (if six or fewer team members are taking part) or to small groups (if seven or more are taking part) and ask them to review the post-its and develop a comprehensive and ordered summary on the appropriate flipchart sheet.

5.   These summaries can then be fed back to the full group in the original order and discussed comprehensively. Following each discussion, establish the agreed answer to each of the six questions posed.

6. Once all sheets have been covered, break into subgroups (ideally three to five team members per group) and ask each group to use the agreed responses to the questions to develop a vision statement. Each team's vision statement should:

   - Present a picture of the desired future
   - Fit with the team's history and culture
   - Be ambitious and inspirational.

7. Once all subgroups have developed their vision statement, they can present them back to the full group. From these presentations, draw out the best phrases/statements, and create an agreed vision for the team.

8. Once you have developed your agreed vision, ask the following four questions and make final changes as required:

   - Is it purposeful: does it articulate an image of the desired future?
   - Is it appropriate: does it fit with the team's history and culture?
   - Is it inspirational: will it encourage enthusiasm and commitment?
   - Is it ambitious: will it cause members of the team to stretch for it?

9. Now use your vision statement to review your current mission statement, strategies, objectives and targets. Ask:

   - Is there internal consistency?
   - Are they taking us effectively towards the achievement of our vision?

10. Finally, in the light of this exercise, answer the following questions:

    - What do we need to do now?
    - When will we do it by?
    - Who will be involved?
    - How will we know we've succeeded?

On completion of this exercise you will have a comprehensive source of information to feed into other activities associated with the team's growth and development.

To expand on some of the ideas discussed here, see Aspiration, External, Jam, Motivation, Scenario and Transition.

W

The essential purpose of **walkabout** is to connect and reframe.

Walkabout

Walkabout *n.* A periodic excursion into the bush. (Australian Aboriginal origin)

I have, on just a few occasions, visited my 'origins'. I've returned to the parts of London I uniquely knew and explored as a child. And I have also revisited other parts that my father showed me as being part of his childhood environment. More recently, I took my children to London for a day to play in the parks and explore the sights of both my father's and my youth. Much has changed, but much has stayed the same – in essence at least. A significant part of this recent trip was taken up with me recounting stories of my childhood, placed in vivid context by having lunch in Pelicci's Café – a significant part of my early years! My children were fascinated by the insights they gained into their deeper 'origins'. My wife has also engaged in this activity with our children, in Whitstable. I get the distinct feeling that we all benefit enormously, both individually and as a family, from these exercises. They reinforce values, provide a sense of continuity and build understanding between the generations.

Indigenous Australians see themselves as being deeply connected with their environment. This is reflected in their tradition of walkabout. When they go on walkabout they perform a repertoire of actions at specific points along their paths. This assists them in framing their lives and purpose from a broader perspective. For some, the focus of their walkabout is their ancestral origins and sense of identity. For others it can be about exploring their future. It can also be about seeking the answer to a problem. Some family groups engage in walkabout with the aim of educating their children by recounting stories and traditions. In this way indigenous Australians are able to preserve their identity amidst overwhelming changes in their social environments. But regardless of whether it is an individual or a family group that is involved, the essential purpose of walkabout is to connect and reframe.

We will begin our exploration of walkabout within the context of the modern organization by considering the work of Peters and Waterman (1982). In their classic text they describe management by walking around or MBWA. Essentially, MBWA is based on the concept that a manager needs to understand what is really going on at the front line – not just view reports in their office. By seeing the actual state of affairs on the ground they can better understand what challenges are being faced and what impact management decisions are having on operational performance. Not only is MBWA aimed at cutting through vertical lines of communication but also at motivating the workforce by suggesting that senior management take an active interest in what is really going on.

Many 21st-century observers argue that this is an old and tired concept that has had its day in a technology-rich and time-poor modern work environment. We can send emails in seconds at the click of a mouse and it's simply too costly, these observers would argue, to be away from our desks or to miss critical meetings. However, many managers to my certain knowledge complain of receiving in excess of a hundred emails per day. How much time must it take to read and respond to all of these? And these same managers also complain that meetings which occupy over 60 per cent of their time are largely taken up with circular arguments and agenda items that have minimal or no impact on their own operations and concerns. So, the counter argument to the modern-day critics is that responding to all those emails and attending all those meetings is eroding our relationships and increasing the distance between managers, customers and work colleagues. And as distance is created in our relationships, so we lose trust and understanding. Is it surprising that customer satisfaction, productivity and staff turnover are the three most common themes in organization development projects?

Today, MBWA is sometimes referred to as Gemba Kaizen (continuous improvement of the workplace), a concept that emphasizes the importance of interpersonal contact and the achievement of harmony between people at all levels in an organization through face-to-face contact and involvement.

We can place the concept of walkabout or Gemba Kaizen within our opening story in a number of ways. The manager's walkabout on her first day at work was clearly intended to help her connect with her new working environment and the people that populate it. Through this initial walkabout she laid the foundations for gaining a good understanding of her new work colleagues, both as individuals and as a team. However, she failed to build on these foundations.

Her second walkabout followed the insight she gained from her holiday in Tunbridge Wells. On her return to Barcelona she connected with the wider environment of the city's parish churches in order to refocus the Gaudi project and ensure it remained fit for purpose. In this case, she did follow through with actions. The appropriateness of these actions will depend upon your take on the STEEPLE analysis presented earlier (see External).

If you are not practising walkabout in your team, and you think you might give it a try, here are eight guiding principles that may aid you in your efforts.

1. Do it to everyone. You may remain in such close contact with your direct reports that walkabout is redundant with them. The real power of the approach lies in the time you spend with those in other levels of the hierarchy. Walk around to see those who work for your direct reports and any others whose work is important to you.

2. Watch and listen. Take in everything. Listen to the words and tone of staff as they speak to you and to each other. In this way, you'll learn a lot about their motivation and their levels of satisfaction. This will also help you to reconnect with your frontline staff and

gain a current understanding of exactly what they are dealing with during a typical working day.

3.   Ask questions. Going walkabout offers you a great opportunity to observe those 'moments of truth' when your team members interact with your clients. Ask them to tell you a little bit about the projects or tasks they are working on. And take care to sound inquisitive rather than intrusive.

4.   Don't be critical. When you witness an incidence of poor practice or performance don't criticize the performer. Acknowledge that most performance issues are systemic in nature and refer to the direct line manager or, if you are the direct line manager, address in a one-to-one at the earliest opportunity – with a problem-solving hat on.

5.   Don't circumvent, or allow others to circumvent, the line. Some staff may take advantage of their direct contact with you to complain about their line manager, either directly or indirectly. Coach them to discuss the issue fully with their direct line manager first. If you have cause to question their line manager's judgement, don't indicate this to the member of staff, but follow it up with the line manager – who may have an alternative story to tell.

6.   Share your vision. The Inuit have a saying about their dog sleds. Roughly translated it says 'The view only changes for the lead dog'. Going on walkabout offers a solid opportunity to share or reinforce your vision for the team.

7.   Bring good news. While on walkabout, share information about recent successes or positive initiatives. This may help to increase the confidence of staff and brighten their outlook. So often what is dissipated through the formal channels of communication is gloom and doom. Neutralize pessimism with your own optimism – while remaining authentic and credible.

8.   From a modest opening effort, work towards going on walkabout as often as you can. This has the potential to indicate to all members of your extended team your interest in them and in their work. And it says you don't consider yourself too busy to spend time being present with your team. Critically, walkabout enables you to stay in touch with what is going on in your team, so by way of a relatively

modest starting point, you might put aside just thirty minutes a week for an investment that may truly integrate you – and your decisions – with your team. However, going on walkabout must be compatible with your leadership style. It should not be forced or just a charade as staff will see through non-authentic behaviour with uncanny accuracy.

Include in your planning for walkabout the capacity to reflect on your journeys. Reflections might be recorded in a diary which can be reviewed just prior to your next walkabout. This will provide continuity to your efforts and facilitate follow-up.

To expand on some of the ideas discussed here, see Coach, Delegate, External, Kaizen and Relationship.

X

 The application of **xenogamy** to organizations has the potential to radically improve performance and success.

Xenogamy

Xenogamy *n.* Another name for cross-fertilization.

 Time spent with Cliff or Sally (my professional colleagues) is always both a pleasure and a source of new thinking. We bounce ideas around, feed off our individual and collective enthusiasms, go 'blue sky' (and 'cloudy sky'), and plant the seeds of new plans, a fair proportion of which mature and become projects. Wow, all this cross-fertilization – and at virtually no direct cost!

I think that one of the key ingredients to these sessions that sometimes produce breakthrough ideas and actions is the high degree of variation in the 'gene pool' of ideas that come together during our encounters. Little of this type of cross-fertilization takes place when I am with those who are very similar to me. In these cases we seem to generate relatively uninspired and weak offspring that add little to the potential of our businesses to thrive.

We explored elsewhere (see Scenario) the application of the law of ecology to organizations, i.e. for an organization to survive its rate of learning has to be at least as great as the rate of change of its environment. The discipline of 'organizational ecology' has provided us with a powerful way to explore how organizations adapt to their environments and to the behaviours of other organizations with which they may compete or collaborate. Organizational ecology provides a range of tools for us to investigate and understand organizational life on many levels. Here we will focus on the concept of cross-fertilization or, to use the formal scientific term, xenogamy.

The application of xenogamy to organizations has the potential to radically improve performance and success. It had its foundations in a concept made popular in the 1980s and 90s – that of benchmarking. Benchmarking is the practice of comparing an organization's performance with that of others. Typically, and most fruitfully, comparisons focus on those practices which matter most to the achievement of business success. And the systematic application of benchmarking offers organizations the opportunity to continuously fine-tune their processes, structures and strategies to changing environmental circumstances. But lest we oversimplify, benchmarking goes beyond simply understanding and copying the practices that lie behind the perceived performance excellence of direct competitors. Were it no more than this, the best we might expect to achieve would be competitive parity rather than competitive advantage. Benchmarking, at its best, seeks superior performance by looking outside of our own sector, making it possible to gain competitive advantage.

The term *benchmark* alludes to a reference point by which performance is compared, i.e. an indicator of what can and is being achieved. The term *benchmarking* refers to the actual activity of establishing benchmarks and best practices. Over the past quarter of a century four types of benchmarking have evolved: strategic, performance, process and functional. Furthermore, benchmarking can involve internal, external or international comparisons. Let's look at each of these in more detail.

Strategic benchmarking is primarily aimed at updating or realigning business strategies that have become dated and/or inappropriate. It involves considering high-level aspects of an organization's attributes such as core competencies, the development of new products or services and improving capabilities for dealing with changes in the external environment. Organizational changes resulting from strategic benchmarking are typically difficult to implement and targeted benefits may take a long time to materialize. An example of strategic benchmarking is to be found in the broadcasting industry's current responses to the challenges associated with alternative means of delivering their programmes, e.g. repeat digital broadcasts, broadband internet, podcasts and mobile communications technologies.

Performance or competitive benchmarking is aimed at assessing relative levels of performance in key areas or activities through comparison with others in the same sector. Data analysis is often undertaken through trade associations or third parties to protect confidentiality and, thereafter, the received data analysis fuels thinking on how gaps in performance can be closed within each participating organization. The UK social housing sector is particularly active in this area, with data gathering and initial analysis being performed by the Tenant Services Authority.

Process benchmarking is aimed at achieving improvements in key processes. Benchmarking partners are sought from best-practice organizations that perform similar work or deliver similar services. An example is collaboration between regional social services departments that develop short-term supportive relationships akin to mentoring. This type of benchmarking often results in quick but relatively unstable benefits, particularly if systemic factors are not taken fully into account.

Functional benchmarking is aimed at identifying high levels of innovation that will create significant competitive advantage. In this instance, organizations look to benchmark with partners drawn from different sectors. An example is an international airline that spent time with a Formula 1 racing team to improve their approach to the quick turnaround of aircraft in passenger terminals, i.e. aircraft 'pit stops'.

Internal benchmarking is aimed at spreading good practices and performance within an organization, e.g. between departments, business units, different operating territories, etc. Three key advantages of internal benchmarking are that access to sensitive data and information is easier to obtain and share, standardized data is often readily available and less time and resources are needed to complete the exercise. However, although there may be fewer barriers to communication, analysis and implementation, real innovation may be lacking. Best-in-class performance is more likely to be found through external benchmarking.

External benchmarking is aimed at uncovering examples of good practice and innovation in other organizations. It provides opportunities for learning from those who are at the leading edge of their practices and performance. This type of benchmarking can take significant time and resource to ensure the comparability of data, the credibility of findings and the development of appropriate recommendations.

International benchmarking is aimed at achieving world-class status. Alternatively it may be necessary to go international if there are insufficient national organizations available against which to benchmark. The globalization of trade, business and service delivery along with advances in information technology is increasing the opportunities for international projects. But these can take great amounts of time and resource to set up and implement, particularly in the first instance. And the results may need careful analysis because of national/cultural differences.

The following list summarizes some of the main returns to be gained from an investment in benchmarking:

- It provides realistic and achievable targets for an organization and/or its component functions (see Goal).

- It challenges complacency (see Jam).

- It helps to identify weak areas and indicates what needs to be done to improve (see Balance).

- It creates an atmosphere conducive to continuous improvement (see Kaizen).

- It allows employees to visualize the improvement which can be a strong motivator for change (see Vision).

- It confirms the belief that there is a need for change and creates a sense of urgency for improvement (see Transition).

In our story, and at an operational level, there was little or no xenogamy, i.e. the stonemasons worked independently of each other with no exchange of ideas or performance practice. Internal performance benchmarking was a clear option here. Indeed, the manager gathered the appropriate core data (see stonemasons' performance data) but failed to capitalize on the potential gains to be enjoyed by bringing the team together and having a discussion and problem-solving session that addressed the issue of variable performance. Each stonemason had their own unique blend of strengths and weaknesses to be explored. If held regularly, team meetings would have the potential to become part of a continuous improvement initiative (see Kaizen). Furthermore, process benchmarking may have added value to the introduction of the new mallets, i.e. it would be useful to know what approach other 'classical' building projects were taking with regard to the use of new materials.

Strategic benchmarking was exemplified through the manager's experiences in Tunbridge Wells and her subsequent study back in Barcelona. This led to a significant change in the strategic direction of the Gaudi project. However, to repeat a point made elsewhere (see External), if the manager had visited some of the great British cathedrals (e.g. York Minster) she would have seen that some of these now combine exhibition, theatre, concert and faith activities in the one venue, creating a rich resource for the wider communities in which they are placed. This is in contrast to the manager's proposed strategy based on a single benchmark partner, i.e. the Trinity Arts and Performance Centre in Tunbridge Wells. Herein lies a warning!

Benchmarking initiatives can be highly complex and resource-intensive, particularly if international external benchmarking is being undertaken. However, to get a feel for the process and what it might deliver for your team, a modest internal benchmarking exercise might be undertaken during a half-day team development event.

1. Open the session by reviewing your team's vision and mission. Thereafter, introduce the concept of benchmarking using the notes in this section and your further research as a guide.

2. Place five flip charts around the walls of your meeting space, with each of the following headings:

    •   Our team's core competencies and capabilities
    •   Our customers and what they expect
    •   Examples of how well we do in meeting our customers' expectations
    •   Things we must get right
    •   What we each do that we might benchmark against one another.

3.   Provide team members with post-it notes and ask them to contribute as many thoughts as possible to each of the flip charts – using one post-it for each thought.

4.   When everyone has run out of ideas, allocate a sheet to each individual (if five or fewer team members are taking part) or to small groups (if six or more are taking part) and ask them to review the post-its and develop a comprehensive and ordered summary on the appropriate flipchart sheet.

5.   These summaries are then fed back to the full group and discussed, and decisions are made as to what will be benchmarked and when, i.e. priorities are established.

6.   The full team, or subgroups of the team, can then explore the transfer of best practice through the use of process descriptions, flow-charting, the review and development of core competencies, etc.

7.   As appropriate, capture learning in the form of revised or new operating procedures, the planning and implementation of further training and development and coaching/mentoring initiatives.

If you have gained value from the team exercise described above, you may wish to stretch your wings a little. By way of a primer, the following 12-point checklist indicates what is involved in the application of benchmarking your team's operations with other teams or organizations.

1.   Identify what to benchmark and select the benchmarking team.

2.   Analyse the relevant internal processes.

3.   Identify teams or organizations to benchmark.

4.   Decide on method(s) of data collection (capitalize on public domain information where possible).

5.   Analyse collected information to establish what other information needs to be obtained.

6.   Establish contacts with benchmark partners and plan visits.

7. Conduct benchmarking visits and establish whether a performance gap exists.

8. Communicate benchmark findings to all stakeholders.

9. Establish agreed targets and action plans.

10. Implement the action plans, measure performance and communicate progress.

11. Recalibrate benchmarks.

12. Return to Step 1.

 To expand on some of the ideas discussed here, see Balance, Goal, Kaizen, Motivation, Vision and Walkabout.

Y

There is a clear logic to maximizing the **yield** you gain from your staff.

Yield

Yield *n.* The profit or return from an investment.

The degree to which I have been able to capitalize on my investment in self-development has evolved over a varied career. My original investment took the form of a few years of structured study (a difficult thing for me!). I capitalized on this within my first two jobs at Shell – two years working in Exploration and Production and then another eight in Research and Development (R&D). After the first couple of years in R&D the job became a breeze and I relaxed and enjoyed the lifestyle which involved marine research projects interspersed with squash, five-a-side football and lots of live music in pubs. However, six years of this was enough for me. Being competitive by nature, I began feeling discontented with seeing my peers slip ahead in the career stakes. This, combined with a feeling that I couldn't see myself working at a laboratory bench for the rest of my working life, prompted some further investment. This took two forms: a push to complete a part-time psychology degree I'd started just for fun, and a push to see what else might be available within Shell, with a focus on their London head office where I perceived the greatest opportunities lay.

I effectively promoted my unique skills and experience and landed a two-year secondment in Shell International's Group Planning function. Here I capitalized on my investment again by contributing to the development of Shell's global business scenarios and to two special projects – 'Accelerating Corporate Learning' and 'Reducing the Environmental Impact of Overseas Operations' – each fascinating in its own way. Also, I invested further in my own development by taking on a series of spontaneous challenges, not least the redesign of Shell's Scenario Planning workshops in the Netherlands (see Delegation).

I could continue with my story of successive investments and capitalizations, but suffice it to say that my own consultancy, coaching and organization development business is my current professional return on investment.

Simply put, the primary task of a leader/manager is to invest in their staff and then seek the highest appropriate return on investment possible from each team member – and the team as a whole. Our explorations within The Knowledge have cast a wide net on many of the things we can do to make the most of the resources we have available to us. And there is a clear logic to maximizing the return you gain from your staff. This logic goes like this:

- Set the broad context for your team's operations by developing a compelling vision (see Vision and Aspiration).

- Establish an agreed mission that brings all team members on board with what the team will do to contribute towards the vision becoming a reality (see Motivation and Delegate).

- Set SMART goals that are clearly linked to the achievement of your mission (see Goal and Balance).

- Develop your staff generously to ensure innovation and change become or remain core competencies in your team (see Lead and Transition).

- Promote authentic communication among all team members to facilitate the ongoing development of relationships (see Relationship and Walkabout).

- Work assertively within good performance management systems to ensure clarity of expectations and the maintenance of the employment contract (see Power and Option).

- Learn from others and continuously seek to add further value (see Kaizen and Xenogamy).

Having presented this logic, you might find a review of the referenced sections, in the order indicated, a fruitful exercise in planning your continued use of this material.

Beyond this suggestion, and in a creative spirit that may add further value to our exploration of Yield, let's look at two alternative uses of the term as may be applied to individuals and teams:

1. Team member yield: a measure of the output per team member employed

2. Maximum sustainable team yield: the greatest long-term performance that can be healthily and safely achieved.

To illustrate the potential value of applying these alternative concepts to your team, let's pay our penultimate visit to the Gaudi Cathedral building project.

If we view the individual yield of each stonemason on an annual basis the results may look surprising. Assuming a working year of 225 days, the target output per stonemason would be 2,250 blocks per year (225 days x 10 blocks per day) at + or − 10mm tolerances. Wayne, taking into account his 24 days sickness absence, and 10 blocks per day production rate, achieved an annual output of 2,010 blocks per year at + or − 10mm tolerances, i.e. an 89 per cent performance target. Payne, taking into account his 5 days sickness absence and 8 blocks per day production rate achieved 1,770 blocks per year manufactured to an over-specification of + or − 5mm tolerances, i.e. a 79 per cent performance target. Jayne achieved 225 x 15 = 3,375 blocks per year to an under-specification of + or − 15mm. This equates to a 150 per cent performance target in terms of volume, but if we assume a 50 per cent time inefficiency, as many of her blocks required reworking, a more realistic estimate of performance might be somewhere around 75 per cent. Sayne's performance stands apart with distinction. With an output of 2,442 blocks per annum, all within the desired tolerance level, his performance was almost 10 per cent over target

By exploring team member yield in this way we can quantify the benefits to be gained by taking action to address performance issues. And many options for action have been explored throughout The Knowledge.

Moving on to the concept of maximum sustainable yield, it is likely that once the basic performance issues had been addressed with each of the stonemasons, and attention had been paid to exploring possible improvements to processes and systems (see Coach, Delegate, Kaizen and Xenogamy) a new performance target of 11 or 12 blocks a day might have been set, along with the allocation of specialist roles and responsibilities that would enrich the work experience of individual team members while capitalizing on their individual capabilities and interests. But any revisions to production performance targets would need to take into account the potential systemic effects of these revisions. For example, the potential desirable systemic effects might include:

- Increased efficiency as individual team members, and the team as a whole, developed a continuous improvement culture

- The enhancement of working relationships as each team member saw colleagues in a new light that emphasized positive individual differences

- The emergence of clearer options for succession planning and job role development that capitalized on diversity.

But the potential undesirable systemic effects might include:

- Increased physical or psychological stress and, thereafter, reduced efficiency and increased sickness absence

- Disruption of working relationships as sources of power and influence change within the team

- Loss of clarity for job roles and, thereafter, problems with routine recruitment and selection procedures.

This second set of potential systemic effects is not to suggest we should avoid setting ever more challenging performance targets or engage in diversity-based management practices. But it does suggest we need to be thoughtful, inclusive and reflective when introducing change, a point explored more thoroughly under Transition, Involvement and Goal.

There are two exercises associated with Yield. The first is an audit of your current performance with respect to the 'clear logic' outlined in the opening narrative to this section. Using the template illustrated in Figure 26 as a guide, take some time out to reflect on your current performance against the actions aimed at increasing individual and team yield. The improvement plan that should emerge from this exercise may benefit from exposure to a coaching exercise on each identified action (see Coach).

Actions aimed at increasing individual and team yield	Current rating (high/med/low) and evidence	Improvement plan (actions you will take)
Develop a compelling vision to set the broad context for your team's operations		
Establish an agreed mission that brings all team members on board		
Set SMART goals that are clearly linked to the achievement of your mission		
Train and develop your staff generously		
Promote authentic communication among all team members		
Work assertively within good performance management systems		
Learn from others and continuously seek to add further value		

Figure 26: An analysis of your team's current yield

The second exercise is based on the potential added value of exploring the concepts of *team member yield* and *maximum sustainable team yield*. In practice, the exercise is complementary to that suggested for team benchmarking and balanced scorecard (see Xenogamy and Balance). Two team sessions are recommended as follows:

Team session 1

1.   Open the session by reviewing your team's vision and mission. Thereafter, introduce the concept of yield using the earlier notes of this section as a guide.

2.   Place three flip charts around the walls of your meeting space, with each of the following questions as headings:

   - What are our known performance outputs (i.e. things we measure)?
   - What else could we measure that would be revealing/ interesting?
   - What measures might we aim to stretch through improved processes/behaviours?

3.   Provide team members with post-it notes and ask them to contribute as many thoughts as possible to each of the flip charts – using one post-it for each thought.

4.   When everyone has run out of ideas, allocate a sheet to each individual (if three or fewer team members are taking part) or to small groups (if four or more are taking part) and ask them to review the post-its and develop a comprehensive and ordered summary on the appropriate flipchart sheet.

5.   These summaries are then fed back to the full group and discussed. The final output from this first session could then be:

   - An agreement on what performance outputs will be measured in future
   - A set of targets associated with each measure
   - An action plan for collecting performance data on an individual and team basis
   - A development plan targeted at each individual and the team as a whole.

Thereafter, the action plan and development plan can be implemented and subsequent team meetings arranged to review the new system and its impact.

Team session 2

6. After an appropriate time delay (say, six months) review the process to date including a summary of development activity completed (flip charts retained from the first session could supplement this review).

7. Present tabulated performance data for the individual team members and the team as a whole.

8. Explore the data presented. Note instances of relatively high and low performance, and then explore the causes of differences.

9. The full team, or subgroups of the team, can then exchange tips for improving personal and team performance and transferring best practice throughout the team.

7. As appropriate, capture learning in the form of:

  •   Revised or new output targets
  •   The planning and implementation of further training and development
  •   Coaching/mentoring initiatives that will extend beyond this second team session.

To expand on some of the ideas discussed here, see Aspiration, Balance, Coach, Delegate, External, Goal, Involvement, Kaizen, Lead, Motivation, Option, Power, Transition, Vision, Walkabout and Xenogamy.

Z

 Zen and the art of cathedral building.

Zen

Zen *n.* A Japanese school of Buddhism.

 A concept from Buddhism that has appealed to me for over two decades is that of the Eightfold Path. This offers a practical framework for development with an emphasis on seeking to see things as they are, rather than as we are!

Throughout my life, reading has been a valuable foundation for my learning. But real learning is about understanding what I've read within the broader context of my daily experiences. So now I invite you to take stock and reflect on your journey so far. As you reflect, you may find yourself seeing things in new ways, correcting old misperceptions, acknowledging hitherto convenient stereotypes and taking new approaches to problems that more effectively engage you with what's really going on.

The aspects of the Buddhist Eightfold Path are not to be interpreted as a sequence of single steps to be followed, but rather as a highly interdependent set of principles that have to be seen in relationship with each other. My take on the Eightfold Path (i.e. the way I have gained inspiration from it), and how it relates to organizational life as I have experienced it, is provided below (Buddhists please accept I may have wandered a little from the path!).

- Right view is about seeing and understanding things as they really are. Since we all have our own window on the world based on past and present experiences, reflecting on the right view is about engaging more productively with the world view of others.

- Right intention is about having integrity in our dealings with our colleagues, our employing organizations and the world in general.

- Right speech is about expressing ourselves in a way that moves us and others forward rather than a way that locks us into old ways of thinking and interacting. What we say can diminish or enhance lives, make enemies or friends, start a war or create peace.

- Right action is about doing things right and doing the right things, a distinction often applied to management vs leadership.

- Right livelihood is about earning our living in a way that we feel maintains our integrity. In essence, it is about having our own personal values aligned with the values of the organization(s) for which we work.

- Right effort is about combining our mental and physical energy in a focused manner in order to achieve our aims.

- Right mindfulness is about seeing things with an uncluttered mind. It's about being aware of self-limiting beliefs and using the right models to make sense of what we observe and experience.

- Right concentration is about the development of our ability to pay attention to what is most important in the here and now.

Figure 27 illustrates the Eightfold Path in relation to three of the key players in our opening story. I have populated this with one possible analysis of how it was for each of these individuals. Taking the analyses as presented, what might you, as manager, have done to facilitate the stonemasons' adjustment to the healthiest possible Eightfold Path for each of them personally? And how well might these adjustments have brought them into alignment with the organization's evolution?

	Wayne	Jayne	The manager
Right view	Wayne was seeing things through his past experiences rather than as they now were in the present.	Jayne had clear views that were aligned with her belief system.	The manager stretched herself to see how things were, but not how people were!
Right intention	Wayne may have had integrity in the past, but was showing none in the present.	Jayne maintained integrity throughout, based on her strongly held beliefs.	The manager maintained personal integrity in her dealings with people – she just didn't understand them.
Right speech	Wayne expressed himself in a way that moved no one.	Jayne had clear views and beliefs, but she didn't try to persuade.	The manager had varying success in expressing herself in a way that moved others.
Right action	Wayne's actions did no more than maintain an uneasy status quo.	Jayne did the right things to maintain her personal integrity.	The manager did the right things – but not in the right way!
Right livelihood	Wayne may have started out earning his living in a way that maintained his integrity – but the latter was now lost.	Jayne was in the right job until it clashed with her values at a strategic level. Then she moved.	The manager continued throughout, to earn her living in a way that maintained her integrity.
Right effort	Wayne's efforts achieved no more than maintaining his employment at the lowest possible cost to himself.	Jayne scored well and was aligned with the organization in the beginning, but became misaligned on strategy.	The manager scored weakly here due to her lack of attention to the belief systems of her stonemasons.
Right mindfulness	Maybe Wayne did see things as they really were at some point in the past but he was now 'locked' in withdrawal.	Jayne was able to see things as they were operationally, but not strategically.	The manager maintained an uncluttered mind operationally and strategically – but failed on the 'human factor'.

Right concentration	It is unclear as to what was important to Wayne, but we may draw our own conclusions from the above!	Jayne never lost her ability to pay attention to the here and now. The clash of strategy was just too great.	The manager failed to grasp what was most important from her stonemasons' perspectives.

Figure 27: Zen and the art of cathedral building

This can be an individual or team exercise. I suggest it be used as both – from time to time. The task is to take some time out for quiet reflection.

1. If you are engaging in an individual exercise find a quiet spot, ideally in some green space at a quiet time of day. The aim is to minimize external distraction and maximize your potential to open your mind to new perspectives. If a team exercise, find a conducive environment (a team retreat might be a great idea, especially if combined with a bit of luxury in the form of a health spa!).

2. Reflect on your team, your organization and your experiences of leadership and management by asking yourself the following questions:

   • What's working well?
   • What do you need to do to nurture these elements (maybe refer back to the components of the Eightfold Path)?
   • What isn't working well and what might be the underlying causes?
   • What do you need to do to improve these elements of your working life?

3. Having noted your answers to these questions, take some further time to review the material in this book with the aim of identifying the exercises that will help nurture what is working well and help address the underlying causes of what isn't working well.

4. It may now be useful to engage in some self-coaching (see Coach), placing your answers to some of the questions posed above into the coaching questions framework as 'Goals'.

This final section is linked to the entire content of The Knowledge, along with all of your own life experiences. It has been my intention that your first pass through the models, concepts and exercises presented in this resource will facilitate your initial steps towards a deeper understanding of, and engagement with, the complex foundations and dynamics of organizational life. Now you have begun this journey I hope you sense that there is a little more going on than is often being seen or understood within your organization. Whether you have or haven't used all the tools and techniques in this book, they remain available to you for your ongoing exploration and application. And my further hope is that you will work back through the material, taking advantage of the links between sections and the 'Metro Map' on the back cover to establish an integrated path towards your future leadership and organization development efforts. As you do this you may gain more confidence in the feeling that you are starting to see things as they really are.

I wish you well in your explorations.

Bibliography and sources

Ambur, O. (2000) *'Reconsidering the Higher-Order Legitimacy of French and Raven's Bases of Social Power in the Information Age'*, Presentation to University of Maryland University College, 15 July 2000.

Ansoff, H.I. (1987) *Corporate Strategy*, Penguin.

Beer, M. (1980) *Organizational Change and Development: A Systems View*, Scott Foresman & Co.

Block, P. (2000) *Flawless Consulting*, Jossey-Bass.

Buckingham, M. and Clifton, D.O. (2004) *Now Discover Your Strengths: How to Develop Your Talents and Those of the People You Manage*, Pocket Books (part of Simon & Schuster UK).

Covey, S. (1989) *The Seven Habits of Highly Effective People*, Simon & Schuster, New York.

Dilts, R.B. (1996) *Visionary Leadership Skills: Creating a World to Which People Want to Belong*, Meta Publications, California.

Edwards, B. (2001) *Drawing on the Right Side of the Brain*, 3rd edn, HarperCollins, London.

French, J.P.R. Jr. and Raven, B. (1986) *'The Bases of Social Power'*, in D. Cartwright and A. Zander (eds), *Group Dynamics*, Harper & Row.

Friedman, M. (2005) *Trying Hard is Not Enough – How to Produce Measurable Improvements for Customers and Communities*, Trafford Publishing.

Gleik, J. (1998) *Chaos: The Amazing Science of the Unpredictable*, Vintage.

Hannan, M.T. and Freeman, J.H. (1989) *Organizational Ecology*, Harvard University Press, Cambridge, MA.

Hersey, P. and Blanchard, K. (1982) *Management of Organizational Behavior: Utilizing Human Resources*, Prentice-Hall, Englewood Cliffs, NJ.

Hollingsworth, M.J. (1999) *'Purpose and Values'*, British Journal of Administrative Management, Jan/Feb.

Kaplan, R.S. and Norton, D.P. (1993) *'Putting the Balanced Scorecard to Work'*, Harvard Business Review, Sep/Oct.

Katz, B. and Docherty, J. (1994) *Enhancing Employee Performance*, Management Books 2000 Ltd.

Kolb, D. (1984) *Experiential Learning: Experience as the Source of Learning and Development*, Prentice-Hall.

Lathem, G. and Locke, E. (2002) *'Building a Practically Useful Theory of Goal Setting and Task Motivation'*, American Psychologist, vol. 57, no. 9, pp. 705–17.

Levine, S. and Crom, M. (1994) *The Leader in You*, Simon & Schuster.

Lewin, K. (1951) *Field Theory in Social Science*, Harper Row, New York.

Locke, E.A. (1996) *'Motivation Through Conscious Goal Setting'*, Applied and Preventive Psychology, vol. 5, pp. 17–24.

Locke, E.A. (2001) *'Motivation by Goal Setting'*, Handbook of Organizational Behaviour, vol. 2, pp. 43–54.

McGregor, D. (1987) *The Human Side of Enterprise*, Penguin.

McNair, C.J. and Leibfried K.H.J. (1992) *Benchmarking: A Tool for Continuous Improvement*, HarperBusiness.

Miller, D.S., Catt, S.E. and Carlson, J.R. (1996) *Fundamentals of Management: A Framework for Excellence*, West Publishing.

Owen, N. (2001) *The Magic of Metaphor*, Crown House Publishing.

Peters, T.J. and Waterman, R.H. (1982) *In Search of Excellence: Lessons from America's Best-Run Companies*, HarperBusiness Essentials.

Pforsich, H. (2005) *'Does Your Scorecard Need a Workshop?'*, Strategic Finance, vol. 86, no. 8, pp. 30–5.

Schwartz, P. (1996) *The Art of the Long View: Planning for the Future in an Uncertain World*, John Wiley & Sons.

Senge, P. (1999) *The Dance of Change*, Nicholas Brealey.

Sherwood, J.J. and Glidewell, J.C. (1973) *'Planned Renegotiation: A Norm-setting OD Intervention'*, The 1973 Annual Handbook for Group Facilitators, Pfeiffer & Co.

Taffinder, P. (1995) *The New Leaders: Achieving Corporate Transformation Through Dynamic Leadership*, Kogan Page.

Tannenbaum, R. and Schmidt, W.H. (1973) *'How to Choose a Leadership Pattern'*, Harvard Business Review, May/June.

ten Have, S., ten Have, W. and Stevens, F., with van der Elst, M. and Pol-Coyne, F. (2003) Key *Management Model: The Management Tools and Practices That Will Improve Your Business*, Pearson Education Ltd.

Treacy, M. and Wiersema, F. (1996) *Discipline of Market Leaders: Choose Your Customers, Narrow Your Focus, Dominate Your Market*, HarperCollins, London.

Turner, S. (2002) *Tools for Success: A Manager's Guide*, McGraw-Hill Professional.

Watson, G. (1993) *Strategic Benchmarking: How To Rate Your Company's Performance Against the World's Best*, John Wiley & Sons.

Whitemore, J. (2009) *Coaching for Performance*, Nicholas Brealey Publishing.

If you or your organization would like to work directly with Carl Taylor on courses related to The Knowledge, or in his capacity as an executive coach or organizational change consultant, please contact:

Direct: +44 (0)7969029314
Office: +44 (0)1622766143

Email: carl@theknowledge.biz
Website: www.theknowledge.biz